A Guest in a Nightmare

A Guest in a Nightmare

Barry Igdaloff

iUniverse, Inc.
New York Bloomington Shanghai

A Guest in a Nightmare

iUniverse books may be ordered through booksellers or by contacting:

iUniverse
1663 Liberty Drive
Bloomington, IN 47403
www.iuniverse.com
1-800-Authors (1-800-288-4677)

Because of the dynamic nature of the Internet, any Web addresses or links contained in this book may have changed since publication and may no longer be valid.

The views expressed in this work are solely those of the author and do not necessarily reflect the views of the publisher, and the publisher hereby disclaims any responsibility for them.

ISBN: 978-0-595-51188-4 (pbk)
ISBN: 978-0-595-61794-4 (ebk)

Printed in the United States of America

Contents

Foreword

Peter Lynch has said that investors should look for companies any idiot could run, because someday one would. Barry Igdaloff's *A Guest in a Nightmare* is just such a cautionary tale. Here is a story of a money manager looking for a superior growth investment for himself and his clients that veers wildly off course. That he made money is irony; the costs incurred along the way are the real story. They serve as a captivating tale of corporate mismanagement and misfeasance, to say nothing of dubious ethics and sexual harassment. As Igdaloff goes from passive investor to active, and then a member of the board, he will guide you through a story of how the fallibility of human nature—the lust for money and power—can permeate the corporate structure. If you've ever wondered how an investment can make you run from the boardroom to the restroom, this is your book. In the end, *A Guest in a Nightmare* is not only an enjoyable ride, but a lesson every investor should learn.

Scott Lasser
Author of ***Battle Creek*** and ***All I Could Get***

1

The Crew

Brad poked his head in my office, "Hey Iggy, I've got Dick Sampson coming in for a lunch meeting with Cliff Stanley from Guest Supply. Will you come? I'm worried I won't get enough guys."

I told him I would, just to help him out. I had no idea that this meeting would lead to an 11 year ordeal that would consume my life. I would come excruciatingly close to professional, financial & emotional ruin.

Brad Dolgin & I grew up in Toledo, Ohio. Despite being in different school districts, we knew each other through Sunday school & playing basketball at the JCC. We became very good friends during our high school years. Much of that time was spent playing cards 15-20 hours per week for some fairly high stakes considering none of us had much money. You could easily win or lose $150 in a night. Not bad for 1971.

After college, Brad spent a few years working for his Dad in the scrap metal business. He then hooked up with the hot local tax shelter syndicator in Toledo. This was a great business in the 80's until the 1986 tax reform bill basically killed the business. Brad then joined a small regional stock brokerage firm. The office manager & Brad's mentor was Dick Sampson. Dick would become the central figure in this story; the primary connection between most of the various characters.

I decided to get into the investment business in 1983. I was working in the International Tax department of Ernst & Whinney in New York City at the time. I was a CPA & also had a law degree. My future with the firm was bright but I was making more money from my stock trading than from my job. My ultimate goal was to accumulate wealth & I believed being in the investment business provided the best opportunity to do so. Of course all of my friends & family thought I was crazy & had lost my mind.

I applied for a stock broker position at Shearson. After taking a battery of tests, they wanted me to be a research analyst. They said the tests showed I had no sales aptitude, one of the lowest scores they'd ever seen. Even though they called their brokers "financial consultants," they viewed them as salesman. The firm would tell you what to sell. I had no interest in being a salesman. I just wanted to trade stocks for my own account. I realized I would need to have some clients but viewed that minor detail as a necessary evil. The goal was to rapidly accumulate wealth and I knew that the after-tax net of a W-2 from client commissions wasn't going to get me there. After being initially hired to work in their Wall Street branch, I decided to return to Columbus, Ohio where I had attended law school at Ohio State & also where I had spent 4 years with Ernst before transferring to New York. My wife & I were thinking about starting a family and we both thought Ohio made more sense. I also thought I would have much more success building a client base there as opposed to New York City.

After Brad got into the business in 1986 we kept in contact more often. As a newcomer to the business, Brad often sought my advice. After all, I was an industry veteran with a whopping 3 years experience. A couple of things constantly came through during these conversations; it was apparent that Brad really thought very highly of his office manager, Dick Sampson. He also kept mentioning this stock, Guest Supply, that Dick was constantly pushing as a sure grand slam.

When the market crashed in October of 1987, Brad was very concerned about his ability to survive in the business as he only had a year and a half under his belt at that point. He also really wanted to get out of Toledo. All of my childhood friends think of Toledo as a declining rust belt economy with no future although very few choose to leave. They just stay and blame Toledo for their lack of success. With these two concerns, Brad approached me about moving to Columbus and the two of us becoming business partners. I thought it was a great idea because we had complimentary skills. Brad had an engaging and outgoing personality that was very suited to obtaining new clients, while I had the experience and educational background necessary to be successful in managing money. In short, Brad was the salesman & he was selling me.

Brad started to have second thoughts about making the move because of his loyalty to Dick Sampson. Dick had hired Brad, taught him the business and took him under his wing. Brad couldn't face having to walk into Dick's office and resign after all Dick had done for him. He felt like he was deserting Dick especially at a time when the markets were really struggling. But Brad finally got up the nerve to do it. In a twist typical of how Wall Street works, Dick told Brad that he was moving to Rhode Island at the end of the week to take a position with another regional firm, Tucker Anthony. Obviously, Dick didn't think twice about abandoning Brad for a better offer. In hindsight, Dick's move should have been no surprise. He was a Wall Street Gypsy; he had a hard time staying anywhere more than two or three years. I am not sure where he was before 1987 but over the next 20 years he would move from Toledo to Rhode Island, to Cleveland, back to Toledo, to D.C., to New Jersey, to Denver & then to New York City.

So Brad moved to Columbus and joined Shearson. I say Shearson because I can't really remember the actual name of the firm at any point in time. I do remember the progression-Shearson Hayden Stone, Shearson American Express, Shearson Lehman American Express, Shearson Lehman Hutton, etc. Today this same firm is called Smith Barney. In late 1989, two things were happening that necessitated some changes. First, Brad and I decided to discontinue our partnership. Even though we were doing well, we could not agree on the financial division of the revenue. Secondly, Shearson was on the verge of bankruptcy and American Express was selling their ownership stake in the firm. Brad and I decided to move to Prudential Bache. Even though we were no longer partners, we made the move together. It's a testament to the strength of our friendship that we remain close friends to this day. Most ex-partners are like ex-spouses; they no longer speak.

One week after we arrived at Pru-Bache in early 1990, the SEC fined the firm $1billion and placed them on 3 years probation for tax shelter sales abuses during the 1980's. I had never sold a tax shelter to any of my clients primarily because I understood how they worked (or didn't work) due to my prior tax experience with Ernst. Needless to say, our timing was poor but we were able to convince most of our clients to move their accounts to our new firm and we survived the scandal.

So that brings us to that fateful morning in March 1990. Guest Supply was too small to be considered a small cap stock. At $5 per share, its market cap at that time was less than $25 million. Companies this small are called micro-caps. Guest was a New Jersey based company that was founded in 1979. They basically invented and controlled the hotel amenity market. Hotel amenities are the little soaps and shampoo bottles you find in virtually every hotel room. Amenities became a marketing tool for the large chains and 'amenity wars" broke out where a chain would try to gain an advantage by offering more and higher quality amenities in their rooms. Besides soap and shampoo amenities expanded to mouthwash, shoe polish, shower caps, and many other items. As the industry expanded, competitors emerged and pricing became more competitive which killed the margins. Guest tried to survive by branching out to Department store sales which turned out to be a disaster. By 1987 the Company lost $6.8 million on sales of only $33 million. Drastic changes were necessary as revenue was declining, banks called the Company's loans, shareholders filed a class action suit and licensing agreements were canceled.

To the Boards credit, they took the necessary steps. The CEO was fired and Cliff Stanley was named the new CEO. Cliff had been with the Company as CFO for 2 ½ years, not exactly a stellar period for the Company. This should have been the first red flag for me, Cliff's involvement with the prior fiasco, but no one was focused on the past. The focus was on the potential turnaround. Definitely a mistake on my part. Prior to coming to Guest, Cliff had had a rather undistinguished career at Johnson & Johnson. But on that day in March 1990, Cliff might as well have been GE's Jack Welch as far as I was concerned. He matter-of-factly laid out his vision for the Company in a way that was very convincing to me. Remember, I was only at the meeting as a favor to Brad. I had heard dozens of CEO's over the years try to explain why their Company was on its way to becoming the next IBM. I walked out of most of those meetings wondering how the guy had become a CEO in the first place. I came into the meeting with Stanley with no reason to believe this dog & pony show would be any different.

Basically, Cliff outlined a plan for the Company to expand its product line beyond amenities to include everything purchased by a hotel. This 'one-stop-shopping" concept meant selling everything from toilet paper, linens & towels to furniture & coffee makers. The total U.S. market for these disposable items sold to hotels was a whopping $2.5 billion per year. And here was Stanley explaining how his tiny little company was going to dominate this market. Guest was the only company that actually manufactured the customized soaps & shampoos and also sold directly to the hotels. Other manufacturers sold only to 3rd party distributors. Stanley felt this was a crucial competitive advantage that could be leveraged into selling all of the other disposable commodity type items needed by the lodging industry. The idea was that the Company already had salesmen and delivery trucks servicing a hotel, so it was a 'simple matter" for those salesmen to sell more than just amenities. In many cases, Guest had exclusive arrangements with large chains such as Marriott which required the individual properties to buy their amenity products from Guest. What better way to get add-on sales from a customer when that customer is required to buy a necessary product from you already. The relationship and contact is already there; this is definitely not a cold sales call!

The second part of the strategy was to maximize the utilization of the Company's manufacturing plant. Cliff realized that the manufacturing volumes for hotel amenities alone were not large enough to cover the fixed costs of operating the plant so he outlined a strategy to do contract manufacturing for third parties. This contract manufacturing was initially a savior but would later become an albatross for the Company.

Part of the implementation of the "one-stop-shopping" concept involved setting up a national distribution network. To speed the process, Guest acquired the Breckenridge Co., a regional distributor, based in Ohio. Dick Sampson discovered the Guest Supply story shortly after this acquisition through a contact he had at Breckenridge. Beginning in late 1987, Dick would spend the next 13 plus years as an unpaid pied piper or ambassador for Guest Supply. Other than a few periods were he became so depressed and withdrawn that he would neither make nor take phone calls, Dick's life would become totally consumed by his Guest investment.

When Dick took the management job in Rhode Island, he hired a young kid by the name of Tom Day as a trainee, just as he had with Brad a couple of years earlier. Tom was a natural for the business. He had the innate ability to take any small bit of information about a company and turn it into a raging positive even if most unbiased observers would deem this information to be a negative development. I never figured out whether he really believed his own spin but I rarely challenged him on it. It usually was in my best interest to let him believe his spin and let him pass it on to others. I think it was a situation where he actually convinced himself of the merits of what he was saying. My belief is that he rarely intentionally tried to mislead anyone although if he had actually bought every share of stock that he said he did, Tom and his clients would have owned over 100% of the outstanding shares! Everyone knew that you had to discount much of what Tom said but we all liked Tom and took it all with a grain of salt. By the time this story ends in 2001, there was probably no one else, not even Dick or I, that spent more of his time on the phone with the various parties involved with Guest Supply. He was constantly in contact with everyone involved including his clients, other investors, money managers, Wall Street trading desks, research analysts, Cliff Stanley and other Company personnel as well as the Company's hotel and contract manufacturing customers. Although Tom Day didn't really have much influence on the ultimate outcome compared to Sampson or myself, it was the prime focus of his life.

Dick was dragging Cliff around the Midwest for a couple of days that week, trying to get him in front of as many money managers as he could based on his numerous contacts in the area. Dick believed that a company's stock price was solely a function of supply and demand based on the fact that there were only a finite number of shares outstanding. In Guest's case that was a relatively small number, only 3.8 million shares. His goal was to get as much of Guest's stock as possible into "strong hands"; i.e. investors that were long term holders. This buying would get the stock out of the "weak hands"; i.e. those holders who were short term traders or those that didn't understand the long term potential of the story and would dump the stock at the first hint of a bad quarter, a margin call or just a better idea for the money. This would eventually limit the number of shares offered for sale at any given time which in turn would cause the stock price to rise as new buyers were looking for stock. Dick's goal was simple; he was always trying to find new buyers and try to keep existing holders from selling their stock. He did this by trying to convince everyone that whatever success the Company was having was only a small step towards what was coming around the corner.

I had a different view. I believed that stocks ultimately trade based on the fundamentals such as earnings, growth rate and potential future growth rate, free cash flow, etc. Dick's supply & demand theory may work in the short run but ultimately stocks trade where they should trade.

There were 7 or 8 brokers at the lunch meeting. A respectable showing given Brad & I had only been at Pru-Bache a couple of months. We barely knew many of the other 25 brokers in the office. These guys generally came to these meetings just for the free lunch. I doubt any of them bought Guest after hearing Stanley's presentation. It certainly wasn't a negative for me that the other guys in the office weren't overwhelmed by the story. Actually I viewed it as a positive. I probably worked with over 100 brokers during the 13 years I spent at Shearson and Pru-Bache and I could probably count on one hand how many of them I would want to manage my money if I was unable to do so myself. Many were great guys and many still remain good friends but I would be very nervous with the vast majority of them being the guardian of my net worth.

I came out of the meeting and immediately started buying the stock for my own personal accounts and for my clients. I personally bought 25,000 shares at around $5 per share over the next 2 or 3 months. It wasn't easy to buy as the daily volume was fairly low. I was somewhat limited in my buying because at the time I was also buying a mortgage REIT by the name of Resource Mortgage (later renamed Dynex Capital). Resource had recently blown up and gone from its $10 IPO price down to under $2. I was buying as much as I could. It eventually went to over $30 four years later but I sold most of mine in the low $20's. My net worth at the end of 1989 was just under $500,000. I had graduated from law school 11 years earlier worth about $25,000. This represents over a 30% average compounded growth rate although this rate is somewhat misleading due to the small initial capital amount. My strategy was to only own 2 or 3 stocks while margining my accounts for the maximum amount of leverage. Obviously a risky strategy but, in my view, the only way to reach my goal. I never bought a stock unless I believed it could at least double or triple over the next 2 or 3 years. There was no room in my portfolio for the large cap blue chip stock trying to grow 15% per year.

2

Treading Water

Two weeks after the meeting with Stanley and Sampson, my wife gave birth to our fourth child, a son. We now had four kids, two girls & two boys. Our fifth and last child, a girl, would arrive a year and a half later in August of 1991, completing our family. The same week our fourth child was born, construction began on our new home which was badly needed to accommodate our rapidly growing family.

Our new home was less than two miles from Les Wexner's newly completed 65,000 square foot mansion. In 1990 Wexner was the wealthiest man in Ohio and remains so to this day. His $2.5 billion net worth was a result of his stock ownership of The Limited Stores which he founded and grew into one of the largest retail chains in the country. Besides the flagship Limited Stores, his empire spawned many other brands over the years including Express, Victoria's Secret, Abercrombie & Fitch, Lane Bryant and Bath & Body Works. He was idolized in the Columbus area not only for his philanthropy but also as a result of creating dozens of millionaires among investors and employees that got in on the ground floor at his Company. I think I read at some point that a $10,000 investment in Limited stock became over $1 million in less than 10 years.

Wexner's sexuality was always the subject of much speculation around Columbus. Was he a homosexual, bisexual or just asexual with his life partner being his business? It didn't help that women's clothing was his prime focus. Miraculously, he moved into his mansion, married a much younger and very attractive Jewish attorney from New York and had four children, all seemingly overnight! The joke around town was that all of this was just the result of estate planning advice from his attorneys. If you have $2.5 billion, it certainly helps to have a much younger wife and four kids to help with your estate planning issues. Many were convinced that there was a fair amount of truth in this "joke."

I did not know Wexner personally but attended many charitable events for local Jewish causes during the 80's and 90's at which he was the guest of honor.

He would give his impassioned speech which usually included his story about his life changing experience of almost dying while getting lost during a blizzard atop a Colorado mountain. During those years, Wexner would donate around $2 million annually to the Columbus Jewish Federation fundraising campaign, about one third of the total raised. It made my measly $3,500 donation seem meaningless until I realized Wexner was only donating less than one tenth of 1 percent of his net worth. My $3,500 was almost ten times as large as his donation when calculated as a percentage of each of our financial worth.

I couldn't have imagined then that the ruthless business practices of Mr. Wexner's Company would become the prime cause of Guest Supply's problems during the late 90's.

As I was starting to accumulate my Guest stock position during the remainder of 1990 and into 1991, the economy was experiencing a mild recession which was exacerbated by the first Gulf War. Hotel occupancy rates are highly sensitive to the performance of the economy. The thing about recessions is that you don't know you're in one until six months after they start. No matter how well Cliff was executing his strategy, it would be almost impossible to show earnings growth with a headwind of declining hotel occupancy rates. To make matters worse, there is usually a 3 to 6 month lag from the end of a recession until occupancy rates start improving.

Despite the economy, the Company was doing relatively well during that time period and was able to post solid quarter over quarter earnings improvements. The stock price wasn't making any progress and was trading back and forth between $3.50 & $7. When the March 1991 quarter came in at a loss of 4 cents per share, the natives were restless. Sampson put together a conference call among many of the large holders including Brad and I, Tom Day and several others. His main purpose was to let everyone vent their frustrations and then get us confident enough in the future performance of the stock so that, at the very least, we wouldn't sell and hopefully would add to our position. I was disappointed that my first year in the stock was somewhat like treading water but I did point out to those on the call that given what the economy was doing, it would have been unrealistic to expect better numbers. In fact, the $.04 loss was a big improvement over the prior year quarterly loss of $.12 per share.

Throughout the remainder of 1991 and continuing for the next couple of years, Brad and I would get a call every month or so from Sampson. Brad would poke his head into my office, "Hey Iggy, Sampson's on the phone; pick up line two and I'll conference you in." Dick would try to make it seem like he was calling as a favor to update us on the latest info on Guest; new national sales contracts, new distribution warehouse openings or potential contract packaging business. Occasionally, he would get Cliff on the phone as well. Brad and I were somewhat ambivalent about these calls. We knew they were really just disguised sales calls; not much different than us calling a client to pitch him on our latest stock idea except in this case, Sampson was the broker and we were the client!

While everyone generally regarded Dick Sampson as a cheerleader for the Company, there was one issue that Dick was very concerned about early on and he would become very vocal and highly critical of Management and the Board. During the dark transition year of 1988, after the Company almost went broke and Stanley took over, the Board took the opportunity, when no one was paying attention, to begin loading the boat on stock options and warrants for not only Management but for all the Board members as well. This largess finally ended in the spring of 1991 once Sampson started making noise. It was too late; the damage had been done. They had issued 1,027,917 options and warrants to themselves. This may not sound that bad but Guest only had 3.9 million shares outstanding. The options and warrants equaled 26% of the total shares outstanding! To make matters worse, much of the total went to outside directors who, as I would later find out, did nothing other than show up to quarterly Board meetings. The exception was Tom Haythe, who also was Guest's general counsel.

Dick was way ahead of me on this issue. He had much more stock than I did at that time. I was concerned but felt helpless to unwind something that was already done. Option grants are a very controversial practice in corporate America. Obviously, shareholders have no objection to making sure that management is adequately incentivized. The theory of options grants is to align the interests of management with those of shareholders. This alignment theory is an absurd myth. In reality, options-laden managements cannot lose money—even if their stock underperforms. Its heads I win—tails no loss. Shareholders can lose lots of money and even if a stock treads water there are tremendous opportunity and carrying costs.

Another problem is the tremendous earnings dilution created from the dramatic increase in the potential number of outstanding shares. What was particularly outrageous with Guest Supply was the fact that in addition to issuing an exorbitant number of options, they also lowered the exercise price on some older options from $7.75 to $4.75 and extended the maturity from 5 years to ten years.

Dick got the Company's attention by writing letters to the Board. By mid 1992, Dick had been heavily invested in Guest for five years, three years longer than me. The turnaround was progressing very well, as the Company was now consistently profitable after the huge losses of the late 80's. Sales had tripled.

Despite all the progress, the stock was basically unchanged since 1987! Dick's letters to the Board were primarily a result of his frustration with the stagnant stock price. Besides the option issue, he was highly critical of the Board and management on many other issues such as a lack of insider purchases, excessive capital expenditures and the resulting high levels of debt on the balance sheet, and the failure of the Company to adequately communicate its strategy and progress. Quite simply, he blamed the Company for the lack of return on his five year investment.

The nearly complete absence of any stock purchases by Management or the Board was particularly irritating. Here we were, buying more and more of the stock primarily based on all the great things Stanley was constantly telling us and yet none of the officers or directors were buying any stock. The lack of insider buying really damaged the Company's credibility in the eyes of investors. I would constantly be asked by clients and other money managers the following; if the stock is so cheap and the potential so huge, why aren't the insiders buying any stock?

I had no good answer to their question. I certainly couldn't tell them there was no need for insiders to buy because they were granted an obscene number of options!

3

The Next Warren Buffett

As we got into 1993, I started to take a more proactive approach as my position size in the stock increased. Also, I had just completed a two year initiative of converting most of my clients to fully discretionary managed accounts. This meant I no longer had to call them each time I wanted to buy or sell something in their account. They paid a quarterly fee instead of commissions and they would receive periodic reports showing their rate of return compared to the S&P 500 index. Essentially I had transitioned from a regular broker to an actual money manager. The big firms reluctantly let their top brokers do this only because they realized they were going to lose their best people if they didn't try an accommodate them. Since I was now a full fledged money manager, I felt I could no longer solely rely on Dick for information on my largest position. I started having frequent conversations directly with Cliff and also began making annual trips to the Company headquarters in New Brunswick, New Jersey.

Rather than attend the meaningless annual shareholder meetings, I would make a separate trip usually in the spring each year. Typically I would fly into Newark early in the morning, spend a couple of hours in Cliff's office, then to lunch. Cliff would take me to a dimly lit Italian restaurant for lunch near the plant in Rahway. He went there regularly but despite the great food, he was a little reluctant to bring me there because two weeks earlier there had been a mob hit a couple of booths over from where we were sitting. A rough neighborhood; just as a Midwesterner would have imagined this part of New Jersey. After lunch he would give me a tour of the manufacturing plant. I'd usually be home by 7pm. With five young kids at home I tried to minimize my business travels.

As a result of these one on one meetings, Cliff and I got to know each other very well. I liked Cliff and had tremendous respect for what he was accomplishing at the Company. It seemed like he was doing everything himself; a one man show. I couldn't figure out how he did it. I really felt fortunate to have him running this little company as I was constantly adding to my position. I did notice some strange things during my visits. I had envisioned a CEO's job at a small company as very hands on, hectic and demanding; always trying to put out fires. The reality when I was there was totally different. As I would sit in his office most of a morning, his phone rarely rang, hardly anybody came in with something that needed his attention immediately and his desk was cleaner than mine had ever been. It seemed odd and certainly didn't mesh with my perception of Cliff as the guy who did everything at the Company.

These were the days before the SEC enacted Regulation FD (fair disclosure) in October, 2000. Even though insider trading was illegal, there were really few rules that prevented companies from selectively disclosing non-public material information to research analysts, mutual funds or large institutional investors. Of course it was illegal for the recipients of this inside information to trade based on it, but proving they received selective disclosure of non-public material information and then traded on it was nearly impossible. To deal with this problem, the SEC came up with Reg FD which basically prohibits companies from selectively disclosing non-public material information. In other words, any disclosure of this material information could only be made if it was made available to all investors at the same time through a press release, an SEC filing or a conference call open to everyone.

I am sure much of what Cliff told me at those meetings would have been a violation of Reg FD, had it been in place then. One edge I felt I had as a money manager was the ability to pick up the phone and speak directly to the CEO of one of these small-cap companies in my portfolio. Try doing that with IBM.

Everyone was extremely disappointed when Guest reported 2nd quarter 1992 earnings of $.08 vs. $.07 the year before. Sales were up 4.9%. Analysts had predicted earnings of $.17 per share. Quite a miss! The hotel industry was having a hard time recovering from the recession. The industry had overbuilt and now was having a difficult time absorbing all of the excess capacity. It was a double whammy; demand was down and supply was up. As properties were struggling to stay open, they skimped on amenity purchases. Many shareholders were tired of hearing excuses and the stock traded as low as $4 7/8 during the later stages of 1992.

$4 7/8 turned out to be the bottom for the stock. The Company would proceed to produce 14 consecutive quarters (3 ½ years) of double digit sales increases including one quarter when sales increased by a whopping 42% over the prior year! The stock was like a coiled up spring and it would go from $4 7/8 to $34.75 over the next three years.

As 1993 progressed and the stock began to move up, I had the feeling that the sky was the limit for this Company. I felt that the strategy Guest had in place was just beginning to scratch the surface of capturing more and more of the $2.5 billion market they served. After all, sales for 1992 were less than $90 million or under 4% of the total market. I was convinced that I was on my way to becoming a wealthy man.

As a former Big 8 tax guy, I was always looking for ways to legally minimize my taxes. I started to think of the eventual estate tax implications of my wealth accumulation goals. I was only 38 years old and I was obsessed with the law of compound interest. I knew the outrageous sums that could be accumulated if given enough years. I also knew that besides foolish investing, the biggest obstacle to accumulating wealth is taxes. I had seen many clients during my days at Ernst & Whinney that had accumulated huge sums but failed to do any estate planning until it was too late or too expensive. The one thing I learned was that it's much easier and cheaper to minimize your eventual estate taxes before you've accumulated huge sums and while you're still young.

In December of 1993 when Guest was trading around $12 ¾, I formed a charitable remainder trust. I donated 45,000 shares of my Guest stock to this trust worth almost $600,000. I was so confident in my financial future that I was willing to irrevocably give away $600,000, which represented almost 25% of my net worth. I wish I could honestly say that charitable intent was my prime motivation but it wasn't. The Columbus Jewish Foundation was named as the charitable beneficiary but they won't receive the trust principal until the last of the income beneficiaries dies. I named my five children as the income beneficiaries. Because of their young ages, the IRS life expectancy tables estimate that actuarially, the last one won't die for over 90 years!

The main motivation was to avoid capital gains taxes and estate taxes on the assets in the trust. The income beneficiaries must receive the income of the trust each year, up to 5%, which is taxable to them. However, Ohio law does not consider capital gains to be income of the trust, only interest and dividends. So my strategy was to grow the trust tax-free as rapidly as possible with non-dividend paying stocks, so no distributions would be required, and then, at some point, switch the assets into income producing investments and start making distributions to the kids. Because of all the tax benefits, my kids will end up netting much more from these eventual distributions than they would have received upon my death had I not set up the charitable trust. I never dreamed there would come a time when I would personally need these assets.

As Guest Supply's stock price moved steadily higher, Sampson and I continued to talk every few days about the latest developments regarding the Company. I am not sure how often Dick spoke to Cliff but I am sure it was at least several times a week. Besides managing a brokerage office and all of the time he spent on Guest, Dick still had time to come up with other stock ideas which he would pass on to all of us during his calls about Guest. Dick would come up with these small unknown and undervalued stocks. They all had a compelling story and Dick was a master at spinning these stories with his low key style.

We all were extremely confident about our ability to pick winning stocks mainly because of our success thus far with Guest. Since Dick was responsible for "discovering" the Guest story, his subsequent ideas carried a great deal of credibility. Ultimately, although Dick had the best intentions, these ideas turned into wonderful tax shelters.

The first was Grossmans, an old line home improvement retailer trying to survive against upstarts Home Depot and Loews. The story was that even if they didn't survive, the real estate under the stores was worth more than the current stock price. Unfortunately, the high cost to close a store ended up eating up any real estate value.

The next one was Corrpro. This Company was the "world leader" in cathodic protection of steel based infrastructure such as bridges, pipelines and underground storage tanks. The idea was that if a company or government spent money now on this process, the structure wouldn't rust and the future replacement costs could be avoided. Unfortunately, politicians and CEO's were more worried about current budgets or earnings and really weren't concerned about saving money five to ten years down the road when they probably wouldn't still be in charge.

The last one was a classic; Nord Resources. Nord's only asset was a mine in Sierra Leone that was the largest and one of the few worldwide sources of titanium oxide or rutile, a strategic mineral with growing demand. Everything was going great until a civil war forced a ten year closure of the mine. It would be another seven years before Dick would call any of us with his latest "home run" idea.

Around this time, Brad decided to move back to Toledo to become partners with Dick Green, a veteran broker in the Toledo Pru-Bache office. Green, who was extremely successful and very highly respected, needed someone to work with him so he could spend more time with his ailing wife. Brad was the perfect fit as he already knew many of Green's clients from having spent most of his life in Toledo. The move was made even easier due to the fact that both were with Pru.

While Brad continued to be interested in Guest Supply because of all the clients he had recommended the stock to over the years, this interest would diminish substantially as the years went by. Even though he probably had very little stock left either personally or for his clients by the end in 2001, I never would forget, for better or worse, that Brad was the original reason for my involvement.

A few months after Brad moved to Toledo, a new broker would join the Columbus Pru office in February of 1993 by the name of Todd Emoff. I first met Todd during our undergraduate days at Indiana University. Todd was two years behind me in the Alpha Epsilon Pi fraternity house. We had some common bonds in that we were among the handful of guys in the house from Ohio and we were both involved with the annual Little 500 Bike Race. I was an alternate rider and coach while Todd would become an all-star rider while almost winning the race his senior year! This was pretty amazing for the Jewish house mainly known for producing the most pre-meds and the highest GPA year after year on campus.

I also had one of the worst days of my life while staying at Todd's house in Dayton during my junior year in March 1975. Indiana's basketball team was undefeated and playing Kentucky in the NCAA regional finals in Dayton. My life revolved around the Indiana basketball team during those years. I had a very lucrative ticket scalping business which was enhanced by Big Ten titles all four of my years and a #1 ranking my junior and senior years.

Despite an injury to one of Indiana's best players, no one was particularly worried about the game. After all Indiana had beaten Kentucky by 30 points earlier in the season. Kentucky would win the game 92–90. I was devastated. Even though the next years team in 1976 would go undefeated (the last team to do so) and be considered one of the best of all time, there is little doubt that a healthy 1975 team was better. To make matters worse, Todd's mom was irate that I never sent her a thank you note for allowing me to stay at her house. I was just trying to put the whole weekend out of my mind.

Todd and I would become much closer friends when he would move to Columbus to also attend law school at Ohio State two years after I had. The following year he would introduce me to my future wife.

I had continued my ticket scalping business during my law school years. Once I began working at Ernst &Whinney, I didn't think it would look too good for the firm's high powered clients to see their CPA scalping tickets outside the basketball arena, so I turned the business over to Emoff. Todd graduated in four years from OSU in 1982 with a joint MBA-JD degree. The day after graduation, he moved to Chicago to become a futures trader in the S&P 500 pit. Needless to say, his parents weren't happy! I just hope my getting him involved in ticket scalping didn't lead him to the futures pits. Other than the dollars involved, there's not much difference between scalping tickets and trading S&P futures.

He spent eleven years in that futures pit; about the maximum anybody could last given the grueling physical toll of the business. On the floor every morning at 7AM just to get a favorable spot until the opening 90 minutes later, then standing all day while screaming and getting shoved by all the aggressive type A brokers in the pits. It didn't help that Todd was relatively small at around 5' 7" with a slight build.

So after eleven years, he called it quits. He had accumulated a fairly sizeable nest egg for all of his efforts. I am not sure if it was more or less than what he expected when he went into the business but most that try to do what he did get wiped out in the first couple of years and have to find a new profession.

We kept in close contact during those years and I was managing his pension account for him. When he left the futures trading pits, he decided he wanted to become a broker, against the advice of myself and other friends he had in the business. Without getting into details, we felt he certainly had a great understanding of the investment world, but thought he lacked the people skills necessary to attract and retain clients. As is typical of Todd, he ignored the advice. He moved his family to Columbus and got a job at IDS, primarily a mutual fund operation where a close friend from Dayton was working. After a couple of months, he realized that mutual funds weren't his thing so I quickly got him hired at Pru.

Throughout the remainder of 1994 and into 1995, Guest's sales growth accelerated. Not just simply double digit growth but up over 30% over the prior year quarter became the norm with the 2nd quarter of 1995 up 42.1%! The stock hovered in the mid teens, certainly much better than the 5–10 range of the early 90's. While the sales growth was phenomenal, the earnings growth was good but not great. The general feeling was that the earnings growth should be greater than the sales growth because we felt the Company had tremendous operating leverage. Operating leverage results from incremental sales above that needed to cover a business's high fixed costs. Once sales volume exceeds the amount needed to break even, earnings growth should be higher than sales growth.

There always seemed to be a good reason why the earnings didn't quite live up to expectations. The prime excuse was inefficiencies due to the plant expansion. While everyone was irritated about the various excuses, we all felt they were just temporary hiccups that would be non-recurring.

At one of our meetings in the spring of 1995, I spent much of the time quizzing Cliff on the potential for dramatic margin improvement once the never ending plant expansion was completed. There was also the new state-of-the-art distribution center under construction a few miles from the plant that would allow the Company to close five small antiquated facilities. It seemed to me that there could be a huge increase in earnings once these projects came on line. Cliff wouldn't commit to specific numbers but he did say he had models of what the numbers could look like that were so phenomenal he "won't even show them to the Board!"

Eventually, the sales growth just became too compelling and the stock broke out of its mid-teen trading range and would hit $34.75 by the end of Q3 of 1995. The price earnings ratio was over 30 times the trailing twelve months earnings of $1.05. It didn't hurt that the research analyst at McDonald & Co., a small Cleveland based regional brokerage firm, came out with a report in August of 1995 predicting that Guest would hit $1 billion in sales within eight years! I had met this analyst a couple of times over the years. A nice guy and fairly intelligent but the thing I remember most is how young he was; I don't think he had started shaving yet! There's no substitute for experience in the investment world.

In October, the Company announced a 3 for 2 stock split. This had the effect of bringing the price down from the low 30's into the low 20's with everyone getting 50% more shares. Sampson had convinced Stanley that this would increase the trading volume and the lower price would attract more investors.

Just as I had with Brad, Todd and I had lunch together most days unless we had a client meeting or some other conflict. Attached to our office building in downtown Columbus was an upscale shopping mall, Columbus City Center. We generally would eat lunch in the mall at one of the dozen or so eateries. The mall contained a Bath & Body Works store which mainly sold all sorts of creams and lotions. This was a fairly new concept owned by Wexner's The Limited. Guest was the primary supplier to these stores, doing the bottling for all the creams and lotions. After Todd and I would finish lunch, we would walk over to the Bath & Body Works store and simply stand and marvel at the four cash registers with customers standing in line six deep at each one just to buy this stuff. It didn't matter what time of day or the season; this store would always be busy.

As 1995 wore on and the stock continued to climb, Emoff wanted to buy more stock for himself and his clients. There was only one problem. Pru placed a restriction on new purchases. Apparently because of the price rise and the number of shares in all of the firms accounts, they started to get nervous about the firm having too large of a position in a small cap stock like Guest. By this time Sampson had moved back to Toledo to run the Pru office there. When you add his position with mine plus Brad and Todd and other brokers around the country, it added up to a pretty big number. I guess Pru was worried about their liability if there was a problem. It made no sense to me but it wasn't the first or last time one of the big Wall Street firms did something I didn't understand. Their research department didn't follow the stock which in their view made them more exposed from their brokers taking such a large position in a small stock they didn't cover.

The bottom line is the firm would allow no more purchases despite all of our calls to New York to try and get the ban lifted. Emoff would bug me every day to no avail. Between Damron's $1 billion prediction and Emoff's desperation to buy the stock, I should have known this could be the top.

As the stock continued to hit new highs in 1995, Sampson & I spent a great deal of time discussing an exit strategy. We certainly weren't anxious to sell but the stock had risen almost seven fold in the 5 ½ years since my first purchase. The size of our position had grown to a ridiculous percentage of our portfolios; well over 50% due to the price rise. Dick and I discussed whether we should start to diversify. Dick would scoff at the idea; he called it "di-worsifying." His thinking went like this; why get into other investments we knew nothing about with the resulting potential for mistakes when we could stay totally in Guest Supply where we knew everything including what time Stanley brushed his teeth every morning. Dick felt that diversifying away from our Guest position would somehow worsen the risk profile of our portfolios. While obviously no finance book ever written would condone that level of portfolio concentration, I also was aware of one key fact; everyone I knew that had made a fortune did so as a result of one concentrated investment. Look no further than Les Wexner for an example of that.

Dick and I realized that obviously our best exit strategy would be for Guest to be eventually acquired by a larger company but we certainly couldn't count on that happening. Selling large amounts in the open market was next to impossible given our large positions and the relatively low average trading volume of the stock. As a result of my discussions with Dick, I drew up a spreadsheet which outlined a plan to dribble out small amounts of stock over several years. Of course the initial sales weren't scheduled to start until the stock hit $30, some 30% above the then current price. I told Emoff where I kept this spreadsheet, in case I got hit by a truck, so he could instruct my widow how to unwind this huge position.

The stock purchase ban was just one of the many frustrations I had with working at a large firm like Pru. Maybe my next book will cover just how screwed up these big Wall Street brokerage houses were. Traditionally, a money manager or broker had to work at one of these firms because they had all the necessary technology. By the mid 90's that was changing. With the advent of affordable PC's and the internet, someone like me could open his own office and use one of the discount shops, like Charles Schwab, to execute the trades and hold all of the client's securities. So in the fall of 1995, I decided to leave Pru and become independent. Financially, it was a no-brainer. I made more money because I kept 100% of the fee charged to my clients instead of getting only 40% from Pru. Because of this I was able to charge my clients a lower fee. I made more money and my clients paid less! My expenses were minimal compared to the 60% cut Pru had been taking.

It took two or three months to get everything in place before I could actually make the move. During that time, I had to make sure that nobody got wind of my plans. This isn't like a normal job where you give your boss two weeks notice. If you did that in the brokerage industry, they'd throw you out on the street while they called all of your clients. It could be a disaster. Timing is crucial in this ridiculous game. Basically, the firms think the clients belong to them and not the broker even though 90% of the clients will tell you their accounts are at a particular firm because of their relationship with the broker.

During this "quiet" period, every time Emoff would ask if I made any progress in getting the Guest purchase ban lifted, I would now tell him we were very close but I couldn't give him any details and he should just be patient. I knew once I left Pru, the ban would be lifted because of all the Guest stock that would transfer out.

Rose Capital would open for business on December 1, 1995. I converted a guest room in my house into an office. No more suit and ties, no more commutes to and from downtown Columbus. I figured I easily gained an extra two hours per day of productivity.

The Pru office manager wished me good luck and the firm offered little resistance. The fact that I didn't move to one of their competitors certainly helped. They really didn't know how to react to someone going out on their own. It was a fairly rare occurrence. They were also thrilled when I told them I was leaving almost half of my clients at Pru with Todd. The accounts I left behind consisted mainly of people that didn't really fit with my discretionary managed equity approach. I also left several that were a pain in the neck and I just had no desire to deal with them anymore. The move provided the perfect opportunity to get rid of them.

As 1995 came to a close with Guest near its high at $22 5/8 after the 3 for 2 split in October, my net worth had soared to a level I never dreamed I would attain at age 41. In the seventeen years since law school, my net worth had compounded at a whopping 36% annual rate. I was convinced I was the next Warren Buffett! I couldn't have imagined that it would be more than seven years until I reached that high-water mark again.

4

A Deal with the Devil

As 1996 began, I was as optimistic as could be. Even though Guest supply's stock price had basically marked time the last three or four months of 1995, I felt the stock would take off again now that the plant expansion was done and the efficiencies started to kick in. There were also analyst comments suggesting that the 1996 Atlanta Olympics and the two political conventions would create enough additional hotel demand to be equivalent to a thirteenth month.

It was unreasonable to expect the stock to move higher until earnings growth started to catch up with the sales, especially after the huge move the stock had made. After all, 32 times trailing twelve month earnings is a pretty lofty multiple for a small-cap distribution company. The stock got ahead of itself and it's perfectly normal to see a pause after a run like that.

I spent a great deal of time coming up with my own earnings projections for the Company. I basically assumed a 25% per year revenue increase going forward and an increase of 125 basis points in the operating margin each year. Operating margin is the operating profit as a percentage of sales. Operating profit is profit computed without regard to interest or taxes. For example, Guest Supply's revenue for the twelve months ending 9/95 was $159 million and the operating margin was 5.6%. For my projections, I assumed sales would be up 25% to $200 million and the margin would increase to 6.85% for the subsequent year.

This methodology would take earnings from $.70 at 9/95(adjusted for the 3/2 split) to $3.20 per share at year-end 9/99. At only 15 times earnings, the stock would go from the low $20's to $50 in just four years. If we could get a 30 multiple, the stock could be 100!

I realized that these numbers sounded like pie in the sky but I really didn't think my assumptions were unrealistic. The 25% per year sales growth was much lower than recent history. The last time the Company had done less than 25% was seven quarters ago. 25% revenue growth would get Guest to $391 million in four years, still only a 15% market share in the $2.5 billion U.S. hotel supply market.

As far as margins, the 125 basis point increase per year would get the Company to a 10.6% operating margin in 1999. I though it was doable considering gross margins had been running in the 23.5% area even with all of the inefficiencies as a result of the plant expansion project.

The plant was shoehorned into a seedy industrial section of Rahway, New Jersey. There was very little parking and I am not sure how the large delivery trucks were able to find the place let alone navigate the narrow streets in the neighborhood around the plant. There were no major highways anywhere nearby. One winter, Guest lost several days of production when the roof caved in due to heavy snow. The Company's headquarters was 20 minutes away in one direction and more troublesome, the new distribution center was 30 minutes away in the opposite direction. To make matters worse, the plant was very poorly configured which hurt efficiency and drove up costs.

Cliff would constantly complain about the plant and continually used its shortcomings as an excuse for any earnings shortfalls. When he was asked why he didn't move to a better facility, his response was that the rent he was paying on his long term lease was so low he couldn't justify moving. I never saw his economic analysis of this claim, if there was one, but I cannot believe it made sense to stay at that location.

The plant expansion project seemed to take forever and I was able to see the resulting chaos first hand on my annual trips to New Jersey. The Company had to rent eighteen huge tanker trucks which were used to hold all of the solutions needed to fill the bottles of lotions and creams for Bath & Body Works as well as the shampoo bottles for the hotel amenity business. These trucks were parked in a makeshift parking lot behind the plant and were connected by huge hoses to the filling lines inside. They needed heated tankers to keep the solutions from freezing during the winter. The daily rental cost for these tankers was off the charts.

I was impressed on my visits with the new state of the art filling machines that were being installed as part of the project. If everything was working correctly, and that's a big IF, each of the four new machines was capable of filling 250 bottles per minute! I would be mesmerized by the speed and complexity of these machines. As I would stand there and watch the filled bottles fly off the end of the line, I didn't see bottles, I saw dollar signs. I would kill time on my flight home by computing the profit potential from these lines. I would multiply 250 X 60 minutes X 20 hours per day X revenue per bottle, etc. The bottom line is that if we had the orders from Bath & Body Works and the plant operated efficiently, Guest Supply would be printing money.

Besides the expected cost savings from the plant project, I also was convinced the Bath & Body Works (BBW) volume would continue to increase rapidly. Being in Columbus, I was well positioned to be on top of BBW's expansion plans. When Wexner finds a concept that works, he doesn't hesitate to roll out as many stores as he can, as rapidly as possible.

Usually one of the biggest obstacles to the rapid expansion of a new retail concept is finding and securing favorable locations. This wasn't a problem for BBW. With The Limited's clout as one of the largest tenants in every upscale mall in America, they were able to secure very favorable locations rather quickly. They had tremendous leverage with mall owners and didn't hesitate to use it. If a mall owner played hardball, he faced the prospect of a 20% vacancy rate. For The Limited, pulling out of a mall wasn't something they wanted to do but wouldn't have any impact on their earnings due to their huge size. In every case, this was a poker game that the malls didn't want to play and BBW got their prime locations.

Another potential obstacle that BBW had to overcome was making sure they had a reliable supplier for all of the creams and lotions that were flying off their shelves. BBW had an 800 number that analysts could call to hear their monthly update of their sales numbers and store openings. They were reporting some of the highest monthly same store sales increases I had ever seen; usually somewhere between 20% and 30%. The store count would go from 213 at 4/30/94 to 750 by the end of 96. By 1998, BBW would have over 1,000 stores. On top of that, Limited had over 800 Victoria's Secret stores that also sold significant volumes of creams and lotions manufactured by Guest Supply. They couldn't afford to have any inventory shortages.

BBW's relationship with Guest Supply during the early 90's couldn't have been better. As BBW was going from zero to over a thousand stores in seven years, it obviously became clear to them that Guest Supply was crucial to their growth plans. They needed to keep Guest happy. They did this in several ways. Guest would receive several "vendor of the year" awards from BBW. They would refer to their key suppliers such as Guest not as just suppliers or vendors but as "partners."

At one point, the BBW CEO asked Cliff to travel to Columbus to meet with Les Wexner himself. Cliff was awestruck. He actually thought the purpose of the meeting was going to be that Wexner wanted to buy Guest Supply! No such luck. Wexner probably had several motives in requesting the meeting. First and foremost, he wanted to make sure that Cliff would have the capacity to handle the huge volume increases that were coming fast and furious. He also wanted to schmooz Stanley to make sure he would be on Board as a "partner" with BBW's ambitious growth plans. Finally, I am sure he just wanted to look Stanley in the eye and figure out who this guy was that was crucial to the success of BBW. In other words, he wanted to get a read on just what he was dealing with and how pliable Stanley would be in succumbing to BBW's demands.

Wexner also told Cliff that he should just ask if there was anything Wexner could do to help Guest increase capacity to handle the BBW volume. Cliff assured Wexner that he would be able to handle the increased volume. Dick and I felt Stanley missed a golden opportunity. At the least, we felt he should have gotten Wexner to fund the huge cost of Guest's plant expansion. This would have given BBW a big incentive to continue directing large order volume to Guest.

Cliff saw it differently. He didn't want any Limited involvement because he thought that would allow them to dictate terms to Guest and could prevent him from diversifying his contract manufacturing business. This was a major error in judgment on Stanley's part.

Cliff didn't think we needed to worry about continuing to get large order volume from BBW. He felt they had no choice. Cliff claimed that there were no other contract manufacturers that could come anywhere near handling the volume that Guest could. He described the industry as a bunch of tiny mom & pop operations with a guy holding a garden hose over an old rusty filling tank. I never challenged this statement and it would turn out to be a big mistake on my part. I would continue to increase my position in the stock mainly based on the premise that BBW would be generating huge volumes of business and Guest would get that business because "there wasn't anybody else capable of handling it."

He went ahead and did the plant expansion necessary to handle the BBW business and saddled Guest's balance sheet with the substantial debt required to fund the project.

What he didn't realize was that he now needed to run very large volumes through the newly expanded plant just to cover his much higher overhead costs. The only way he was going to breakeven in that plant was to get large order volumes from BBW. So his desire to maintain his independence by not getting funding from Limited didn't work. He was still totally dependent on their order flow.

The gravest error Stanley made was failing to get a binding contract with volume and pricing guarantees from BBW *before* he took on all of that debt to expand the plant. Of all the decisions Stanley made, this was by far the worst and most costly.

The original business plan, when Stanley took over in 1988, acknowledged that the plant was too large to breakeven on hotel amenity business alone and therefore the Company would need to add some contract manufacturing business to help cover the cost of operating the plant. Now, because of the cost of expanding the plant, Guest needed to do huge volumes of contract manufacturing business just to cover the much greater overhead costs.

5

Cockroaches

1996 began well with the announcement that Gene Biber had been hired to replace Jim Reisenberg as VP of manufacturing. This was great news as most people close to the Company felt that the volume and complexity of Guest's manufacturing operation had grown beyond the capability of the retirement age Reisenberg. Stanley and other Board members would frequently use Reisenberg as a whipping boy for the problems at the plant. Biber had extensive experience in high volume manufacturing operations. We all felt Biber would be the answer to our prayers and finally be able to get the plant operating efficiently.

On January 9th, Guest took the unusual step of pre-releasing the 12/31/95 quarterly earnings. They did this because even though sales were expected to be up 27% for the quarter, the earnings were only expected to be $.13 vs. $.11 the prior year. This was $.02 short of analyst estimates. The press release blamed the shortfall on "inefficiencies related to raw materials movement." Basically, they couldn't figure out where anything was in their six local warehouses.

The manufacturing volume growth had been so rapid that it caused gridlock in their logistics. Having six separate warehouses, none of which were adjacent to the plant, resulted in chaos. Consolidation into the new state of the art distribution center would hopefully solve the problem but that was at least nine months away.

Even though the Company's announcement indicated the March quarter would also be a couple of cents below estimates due to these problems, they still expected to hit the 9/30/96 estimate of $.90 vs. $.70 the prior year. Most viewed the problem as a short term hiccup attributed to having too much business and one that was eminently fixable.

While the January 9th announcement was viewed as a minor short-term blip, the announcement that came less than two months later on March 5th was a bombshell. We could live with an earnings miss of a couple of cents but this press release warned that the March quarter was expected to come in at a *loss* of $.13.

After the January announcement, the analyst, Rob Damron at McDonald & Co. had revised his March estimate down to a profit of $.11 vs. $.10 the prior year. Going from a plus $.11 to a negative $.13 isn't a miss, it's a catastrophe.

Too make matters worse, the Company announced it expected the June quarter to be even with the prior year earnings of $.19 versus the $.27 estimate.

Cliff was becoming a master at explaining the various reasons for missed estimates. This time it was a sudden unanticipated deferral in orders form "a significant contract packaging customer."

Cliff would never publicly blame BBW by name for any earnings problem at the Company. In fact, I think the standard vendor agreement BBW had with their suppliers prohibited the public mention of Bath & Body Works. They were trying to maintain the marketing illusion that all of these pure bottles of creams and lotions came from the little 100 year old house in New Albany, Ohio which was the mythical Company headquarters. If it had become common knowledge that this stuff was bottled by Guest Supply in that hell-hole plant in Rahway, NJ, I don't think BBW would be the company they are today.

Needless to say, the stock price didn't take the news well. After starting the year at its high of $22 5/8, the price would get cut in half down to $11 ¼. The day after the March 5th announcement, the stock plunged $6 3/8 in one day! I think it would have been worse had many of the long time large holders not used the weakness to add to our positions.

I was getting ready to mail my first quarterly reports to my clients since I had left Pru and became independent. I dreaded having to show disastrous numbers in my first quarter. Even though I had trounced the market averages for the prior five years, that was considered ancient history when your largest position declines 50% in one quarter. I had to do a great deal of hand holding but I only lost one client. The guy just couldn't stomach the volatility. I can't say I blame him.

Besides trying to reassure my clients, the phone calls with Sampson, Day, Emoff, etc. became extremely frequent; sometimes hourly with the stock in a virtual freefall. We were shell shocked. Over the prior six years, there had been many minor disappointments, but nothing like this.

By far the biggest bone of contention between Stanley and the major shareholders was the issue of stock buybacks by the Company. There were several reasons that we felt it was imperative that the Company aggressively make open market purchases when the stock was in free fall following one of these major negative earnings surprises.

Besides the obvious future benefit to earnings per share by reducing the number of shares outstanding, it also helped alleviate the pressure from margin calls and angry clients. It was a simple equation for me; if Management thought the problems were temporary, it was a golden opportunity. By not buying back stock, it signaled to me that maybe the problems were not as temporary as we were being led to believe.

The Company would constantly come up with excuses to delay buying back stock. When they finally got their act together, it was too late and the opportunity was missed due to a partial recovery in the stock price. Todd Emoff was one of the most vocal proponents regarding this issue. Here is an excerpt from one of the many letters he wrote to Stanley, this one was from May of 1997:

Mr. Clifford Stanley   May 30, 1997
Guest Supply, Inc.
4301 U.S. Highway One
Monmouth Junction, N.J.
08852—0902

Dear Mr. Stanley,

It was nice speaking to you (Paul) yesterday regarding financial matters at Guest Supply, specifically regarding the merits of a stock repurchase. i am writing today in response to one of our points of discussion concerning whether the effects of a buyback are material since the example I detailed in my previous letter showed how it would raise earnings per share by $.01. But that is only in the first year. Allow me to illustrate how the compounding works. Using the same assumptions as in my previous letter, incurring a permanent interest cost of $160,000 per year, reducing shares outstanding from 7MM to 6.75MM.
<u>Scenario</u> I as is 7MM shares
pre tax profit net EPS
year 5 $25,000,000 $16,250,000 $2.32

<u>Scenario II with modest share buyback 6.75MM shares</u>
pre tax profit net EPS
year 5 $24,840,000 $16,146,000 $2.39

Which earnings per share schedule looks better? Which scenario is going to result in a higher stock price five years from now? The answer is obvious of course, and I am not trying to insult your intelligence by posing the question but am trying to point out my frustration with the fact that this action is not already under way.

Let me put this in a different light. The alternative way to get $.07 more EPS in year 5 would be to make an extra $.07 x 7MM net profit or $490,000. Assuming a 4% net margin, that would require $12,250,000 more incremental sales. I respectfully submit that it would be infinitely easier to execute a 250,000 share *repurchase over the next few months than to increase sales by more than $12 million above already planned sales levels. Ask any shareholders opposing the buyback if they will deliver $12 million profitable sales to the company five years hence.*

Here is a follow-up letter sent by Todd 3 ½ months later:

Clifford Stanley Sept. 11, 1997
Guest Supply, Inc.
4301 U.S. Highway One
Monmouth Junction, N.J.
08852—0902

Dear Mr. Stanley,

I was happy to see the August 4th announcement that Guest Supply has decided to initiate a repurchase program of 5% of the company's outstanding conunmon stock. I am however somewhat puzzled and upset about the timing of this action. When the stock price of Guest was in the $8 to $10 area (where it languished for over 9 weeks during May/June and more than 1,195,000 shares traded) the company took no action to repurchase shares. Then, after the stock started trading above $11 in August the company decides to buy back shares. Now the share price is over $13 and to my knowledge no shares have been repurchased yet. The optimal time to buy back shares was May. The entire 300,000 share program could have been completed by now. What is especially upsetting is it could have been completed at less cost and thus to a greater benefit to long term shareholders. I have held Guest stock for many years, hopefully I will be a shareholder for many more years as I see that the company has great potential. The poor handling and timing of this share repurchase can only be regarded as a slap in the face to all long term shareholders. It has greatly upset me that the financial interest of long term shareholders has been ignored in this manner. I think a share repurchase at this time would still be a good thing for shareholders and I look forward to the initiation and completion of this program as soon as possible. However, it is patently obvious that a properly timed and executed share repurchase would have been of far greater benefit to long term shareholders. The benefits would even have compounded over time for those who maintained ownership in Guest the longest. The concept of this share repurchase, done properly, is an easy one to understand. Only one conclusion can be reached. You have failed to optimize shareholder value in this company.

Sincerely,

Todd Emoff

cc: Board of Directors

It was apparent to all of us that Stanley and the Board had no interest in buying back stock to help out the major shareholders. In fact, many of us felt they would prefer that we just sold our stock so they wouldn't have to deal with us anymore. Their tune would change drastically when the buyback issue started to impact them personally, as their options granted ten years earlier started to come due.

One person I spoke to every few weeks or so during this time period was Gordy Morse. Gordy grew up in my neighborhood back in Toledo but was five or six years younger than I was. I got to know him when he was Brad Dolgin's underling while Brad was working at the tax shelter syndicator during the mid-80's in Toledo.

Now, Gordy was pulling down huge bucks as manager of the Atlanta, Georgia Bear Stearns office. Bear Stearns didn't have many offices but the ones they did have were manned by nothing but huge producers and the managers of these offices were very well compensated. Brad and I were always somewhat amazed how Gordy, the little brat from the neighborhood, ended up doing so well. We also knew how difficult it was to keep these huge producers happy and if Gordy could do it, we figured he deserved the money.

Gordy owned some Guest Supply stock so he would call me whenever there was a news release from the Company. After the January earnings announcement, I told him that I had tremendous confidence in Stanley and reminded Gordy that Cliff had been the one to turn the Company around after the disastrous performance under the prior management. Gordy interrupted me to tell me something simple but brilliant that I had never thought of. He said, "Maybe Stanley was the right guy to get the Company from point A to point B, but lacked the skills necessary to get Guest from point B to point C."

I had always thought that you're either a good CEO or your not; either you know what you're doing or you don't. I still believed that Cliff was the right guy but a seed was planted in the back of my mind as a result of Gordy's comment.

I also learned a second tidbit from Gordy when I expressed my frustration to him about the violent price drop by the stock after the March 5th announcement of the BBW order deferral. I couldn't understand why the stock would drop so much and so quickly on news of what I considered to be a short term problem; a one time event that was in the process of being fixed and therefore should be non-recurring. He explained matter of factly that it was due to "the cockroach theory."

Gordy told me that institutional money managers routinely sell their entire position in a stock on the first inkling of seemingly inconsequential negative news from a company. Their theory is that this negative news, "the first cockroach", is just the beginning of a stream of problems to be announced down the road. When you turn the light on in your kitchen and you see a cockroach scurry across the floor, you know that's not the only one. You can't yet see the others, but sooner or later you will.

The money managers sell first and ask questions later. If they become convinced there are no more cockroaches hiding, they can always buy the stock again.

I am sure Gordy followed the cockroach rule and immediately sold his Guest stock. I didn't talk to Gordy as much after that but I remember those two insights he gave me. I had never thought of Gordy as a guru that I would look to for brilliant investing insights but those two particularly stand out in my mind. They both turned out to be right on target as they related to Guest Supply. Even though I didn't know it then, there **were** more cockroaches and Cliff Stanley was the **wrong** guy.

6

The Wexner Squeeze Play

The remainder of 1996 saw tremendous volatility in Guest Supply's stock price. After hitting the low point of $11 ¼ following the March 5th announcement, the stock would rally back up to $17 ¼ by the end of June. When the 6/30 earnings were announced in July, the stock would head back down to below $12. Even though the earnings came in as expected after the prior downward revisions, the sales were up only 8.6%. After 14 quarters of phenomenal revenue increases, we now had two consecutive quarters of single digit increases.

The 9/30 quarter would be another disappointment with earnings of $.22 versus the estimate of $.35 and $.30 the prior year. The excuse this time was a $650,000 inventory write down and an $850,000 "pricing adjustment."

This "pricing adjustment" turned out to be an ultimatum by BBW for Guest to lower its prices if it wanted to be assured of large product orders in the future. A few months earlier, I had received a call from one of the brokers I used to work with in the Pru office. He had just had lunch with one of his clients who happened to be a low level executive at BBW. The client said that Guest was going to lose the entire BBW contract. I told the broker this couldn't be true as Stanley was constantly telling me he was receiving larger and larger orders from BBW.

After I hung up the phone with the broker, I was in a total panic so I immediately called Cliff. He was in a meeting but I told his secretary that I really needed to talk to him and convinced her to get him out of the meeting. Cliff assured me that Guest wasn't in any danger of losing the business and that there was no basis at all to the rumor. Four years later, I would learn that there was some truth to the story and that Cliff was forced to make drastic price concessions in order to keep the business.

Living in Columbus, I was well aware of some of The Limited's unscrupulous business practices. Several of my clients would question our continual purchases of Guest Supply stock once they learned of the Company's heavy dependence on orders from The Limited's Bath & Body Works subsidiary. Their concern was based on The Limited's treatment of their suppliers. They would relate stories of how Wexner's Company would give a supplier so much business that the supplier would become totally dependent on those orders to survive. Once the supplier became dependent on The Limited, the supplier would be hit with demands for price concessions. At that point, most suppliers had no choice but to accede to the demands.

I addressed this concern directly with Stanley. His response was that he had heard the stories but they all related to The Limited's main business which was clothing. He insisted that Guest was immune to this tactic because there simply was no other contract manufacturer that had the capacity to handle BBW's volume of orders. He reiterated his depiction of the industry as "a bunch of mom & pop operations with a guy holding a garden hose above a mixing tank." That image stuck in my mind to my detriment.

It turned out that there were plenty of other contract manufacturers ready, willing and able to handle BBW's business. BBW had Stanley right where it wanted him. Had he not spent a fortune upgrading and expanding the plant, he might have had a chance but he had walked right into the trap. With the shareholders and his bankers breathing down his neck, he had no choice but to do whatever was necessary to keep the BBW business, no matter the cost.

BBW would summon their top suppliers to Columbus for periodic meetings to tell them what pricing they demanded going forward. Cliff related a story to Dick Sampson that at one of these meetings, one of the suppliers took his keys out of his pocket and handed them to the BBW executive stating that if this is going to be the pricing, I am out of business. I am sure the guy at some point had received one of BBW's "vendor of the year" awards as a memento of his experience!

I would also hear stories of BBW refusing to pay some of Guest's invoices based on some bogus claim that was impossible to substantiate. This usually happened near the end of a quarter when they needed to hit some earnings target. What a great way to lower your costs. What could Guest do; they had to bite the bullet.

As despicable as the business practices of Wexner's companies were, it was gross incompetence for Stanley to have allowed Guest Supply to be put in this situation. He had been warned by me regarding their business practices. Sampson had implored him to get a contract guaranteeing pricing and volume or funding for the plant expansion from Wexner when he had the chance.

The Company's stock price was locked in a classic battle between those of us who still believed in Stanley's ability to unlock the promised earnings potential of

Guest Supply versus those who had thrown in the towel after the string of disappointments.

Every time the stock price would falter, those of us who still believed would step in and start buying, causing the price to rebound. The result was that my position was getting larger and larger. It was getting to the point where I couldn't have sold it if I wanted to. I had too many shares and the trading volume was diminishing. I was no longer just a stockholder; I was now a "stuckholder."

By year end, the bulls had gained the upper hand. Despite the slowing sales growth and the gridlock at the plant, the stock would close the year at $17 5/8. Still down $5 for the year but a respectable showing given that the earnings came in at only $.45 for the year versus the $.90 estimate and $.70 the prior year. Throw in the three consecutive quarters of only single digit sales growth and I was thrilled to get out of the year with a $17 5/8 stock price. After these results, a good argument could have been made that the stock was worth only $9 or $10 based on the fundamentals.

Heading into 1997, I was confident that the seemingly endless problems of 1996 were behind us. With the stock moving higher, the plant project finally done and the new distribution center nearing completion, there was good reason for optimism.

As a result of my additional stock purchases during the prior year sell-offs, my clients and I now owned 513,287 shares of Guest Supply. This amounted to an 8.6% stake in the Company. As an owner of over 5% at year end, SEC rules required me to file a Form 13G to publicly report my holdings. A Form 13G is used by passive institutional investors that have accumulated over 5% in the ordinary course of their business without the intent to change or influence control over the company.

I was glad I had to do the filing. While Cliff knew I was a large holder, I think he was somewhat shocked by the size of my position. Despite all of the problems, I was still on very good terms with Cliff but I am sure he became a little concerned in the back of his mind, especially when he knew Dick Sampson, Tom Day & others also had large positions.

Guest reported $.17 earnings for the 12/96 quarter, the first time in over a year that the Company met analyst estimates. This was a slight improvement over the prior year's $.13 number and sales growth started to accelerate again with a 14% increase.

When the annual report and proxy material arrived in the mail in late January, I was surprised to see that the old stock option issue had reared its ugly head again, especially after the disastrous year we had just been through. They granted

160,000 additional options at a strike price of $15.25 which was $7.50 below the stock price at the beginning of the year. At least no options were granted to the outside directors this time.

Dick felt it was time to write another one of his letters but this time he felt I should send it instead of him. He felt it might have more impact coming from me as a result of my recent 13G filing. Dick faxed me his draft and I typed it up and sent it to the Board. Below is a copy of the letter.

February 5, 1997

Board of Directors
Guest Supply, Inc.
4301 U.S. Highway One
P.O. Box 902
Monmouth Junction, NJ 08852-0902

As a longtime major shareholder of the Company, I am writing to ask the Board to act on the following items.

1. 1996 Stock Option Grants

I strongly encourage the use of stock options to reward and/or create incentive for management. The Board in the past has justly rewarded management and adjusted exercise prices where it felt appropriate. However stock dilution hurts, especially in light of poor earnings results and must be carefully considered. We all know that 1996 was a transitional year for the Company when much was accomplished. However earnings declined 35% with a like drop in the value of the share price, in fact the stock dropped almost 50% in value at one point. I believe the large capital outlays over the past two years will begin to show the returns that have long been anticipated. Nevertheless, the stock has greatly underperformed all indices, especially industry comparisons. In no case should management benefit because shareholders had a bad year or the company had a bad year. In over 19 years as an investor, I am not aware of any company with similar results granting this amount of options to long-time employees, especially at an exercise price $7.50 below the price on 1/1/96 in a year when the general market was up over 20%. If the stock just gets back to where it was on 1/1/96 this would equal $1.2 million of additional compensation in a year when the entire Company's profit only equaled $3.2million. I believe the exercise price of $15.25 constitutes a windfall to option recipients. This has enraged many longtime shareholders including myself. At the very least this exercise price should be immediately changed to $20 per share.

2. Stock <u>Buyback</u>

Providing the Board agrees that the capital investments of the past two years are still going to generate the expected benefits, the Company should institute an immediate stock buyback program. This is not at all uncommon for companies, both large and small, that believe the price of the stock does not adequately reflect future expectations. In other words, sometimes it is in the best interests of shareholders for the Company to buy their own stock because it represents very high rates of return when compared to alternative uses of capital. We are convinced that a stock buyback program at current prices represents excellent value and will result in a higher stock price. Higher stock prices are beneficial in many ways including providing "tender" for future company growth through expansion or acquisition.

3.<u>StockOwnership</u>

The Board of Directors of Guest Supply, except on rare occasions, have been conspicuously absent from open market purchases of the stock. Shareholders of the Company believe strongly that Board ownership is very important to serving the needs of shareholders. It creates confidence among investors enabling them to purchase or continue to hold stock in the Company. Potential investors have trouble understanding why they should purchase stock when the Board members don't do so.

I believe the future is bright for Guest Supply, however the shareholder's list has lost some large institutional investors including RCM, Palisades and Columbia representing well over one million shares. It is time for the Board to protect shareholder's interests and act on the above items.

Sincerely,

Barry Igdaloff

I received no response to my letter.

I made my annual visit to New Jersey in late March of 1997. I was looking forward to the trip because the new distribution center was finally done. I had heard so much about how phenomenal it was with its automated systems and 250,000 square feet. This facility was absolutely crucial to the success of the Company and I was anxious to see it for the first time.

Despite the letter, Cliff and I were still on good terms. Our meeting went well but Cliff seemed tired and stressed out. He had gained quite a bit of weight since I had seen him a year earlier. As we had done in prior years, we had lunch but instead of going to the plant, Cliff was going to give me a tour of the new distribution center. Since I had no clue where I was going, the plan was for me to follow Cliff in my rental car so I could head to the airport after the tour. As I was following Cliff, I could see he spent several minutes talking on his cell phone. I didn't think anything of it at the time. After about twenty minutes of driving we arrived at our destination, except we were at the plant, not the distribution center. I was bewildered as Cliff explained that things were too busy at the distribution center that day and he felt our time would be better spent at the plant.

I was confused and somewhat irritated but accepted Cliff's "explanation" at face value. I didn't think of the incident again until the news release hit my screen about a month later on April 25, 1997. Despite a 19% sales increase, the Company announced it had a *loss* of $.21 for the 3/97 quarter. The culprit this time was a $2.2 million inventory write off as a result of "damaged, obsolete, and below standard inventory identified during the recent consolidation of the company's seven warehouses to its new distribution facility." In addition they had $426,000 in extra costs incurred to move everything to the new facility.

My strong suspicion is that as I was following Cliff to the new distribution center a month earlier, his cell phone call on the way alerted him to the fact that the auditors were there, tallying up the carnage, and maybe this wouldn't be a good time to give your largest shareholder a tour of the new facility!

After starting the year at $17 5/8, this announcement would cause the stock price to plummet again down to $8 ¾ by June. Sampson and I made a panicked conference call to Stanley. Besides demanding that the Company immediately initiate a share buyback program to support the falling price, we strongly suggested that Stanley add both of us to the Company's Board of Directors pronto.

We both felt that since we were the Company's largest shareholders, we should be represented on the Board. We certainly had no confidence that the existing Board would take the necessary steps to save this sinking ship. If they had owned material amounts of stock we might have felt differently.

Surprisingly, while Stanley didn't exactly promise us the seats, he did say he would try to get it done. As we pressed him on it over the next few days, he began to hedge. My guess is that he encountered strong resistance from the Board, especially Tom Haythe. Stanley tried to buy himself time by suggesting that we try to come up with some board candidates with industry experience that might be able to help the Company operationally. I knew he was just trying to drag out the discussion until the next earnings release in July. If he could report a decent number, maybe we would all calm down.

Regarding the stock buyback issue, the Company took no action. The shareholders were enraged. The general feeling was that if the Company didn't think the stock was a bargain at $8 ¾, our problems were much more serious than anyone had imagined. Cliff claimed that the Company's banks wouldn't allow any buybacks. Cliff always had an excuse.

I spent the month of May trying to keep my clients from either, forcing me to sell their stock or moving their accounts altogether. I also had to scramble to deal with margin calls in my own account as a result of the price drop. I dreaded turning on my computer each morning for fear I would see notice of another account transferring out. Easily the most difficult month of my career.

Luckily, when our five kids got out of school in early June, we went on our previously planned trip out west, visiting several national parks. I am not sure I could have survived the Guest ordeal without the kids. They were my prime motivation to persevere. No matter what was happening, good or bad, with my investments, I tried to keep an even keel with my family. I never mentioned any of the Guest problems. As far as they knew, everything was normal. I knew that wasn't the case. If the stock dropped much further, margin calls would have forced me to start selling. This selling would have caused the price to go lower creating more margin calls and more forced selling, etc.

The bottom line is I could easily have been totally wiped out financially. My wife would have been forced to find a job instead of caring for the kids. We would have had to sell the house and move into a more modest home. On top of all this, I worried about lawsuits. An attorney wouldn't have to be that sharp to find a reason to sue; over concentration or lack of proper diversification would have been layups. I couldn't resist adding to positions during the prior year sell-offs and the result was many accounts with 30% to 40% in Guest Supply. This problem was exacerbated when clients withdrew money from their accounts which had the effect of increasing the Guest Supply weighting. Throw in the ubiquitous claim of "unsuitability" and any decent plaintiff's attorney would have a field day.

I had though about getting liability insurance when I went independent in late 1995 primarily due to the large Guest Supply position. I decided against it since most of my clients already owned Guest at that point and I didn't think a liability policy would protect me on an existing position. Miraculously, although I ended up losing many of my clients due to the problems at Guest, I never was sued.

I contemplated having to switch professions if my client base kept shrinking due to the stock drop. I thought about getting back into tax accounting after fifteen years. With five kids under fourteen, the pressure was enormous. The trip enabled me to get my mind off of my Guest Supply problems. Not totally, but I did the best I could.

I wonder if Stanley knew what we were going through when Dick and I made the panicked call demanding a stock buyback and board seats.

7

Chicago Mink Oil

I was exhausted after a along but exhilarating day with my family at Zion National Park. As I plopped down on the bed of my room in the finest and only motel in Panguitch, Utah, I dreaded what I now needed to do; call my office answering machine to retrieve the day's messages. This is normally a routine task when I am out of the office but given what Guest Supply's stock price had done over the last six weeks, I didn't look forward to hearing from any of my clients.

On this particular day, I got a message from my brother in-law, Manny Roth. Manny didn't call often and he knew I was on vacation in the middle of nowhere, so his message for me to call him back, as soon as possible, was unusual to say the least.

Manny was married to my wife's sister and he was easily one of my favorite people in my wife's large extended family. Manny was retired from an executive position with Rich's department store; an Atlanta based regional chain that was part of the Federated department store group.

One of Manny's roles at Rich's was being in charge of the cosmetics division. In that role he became good friends with Bob Shapiro, the owner of a Chicago based cosmetics company named Emlin Cosmetics. Emlin only made high-end skin care products that were primarily carried in stores such as Nieman Marcus. Emlin also had the exclusive contract to supply all Hyatt hotels with a luxury amenity package for their rooms.

Even after Manny retired, Bob Shapiro would still take Manny out to lunch or dinner or to a Braves game every time he was in Atlanta. One of those meetings occurred while I was on vacation in Utah. Apparently, Shapiro mentioned off-hand to Manny that he was really interested in a hotel amenity company that had just had a big price drop. Manny's eyes lit up as he personally owned some Guest and knew the situation well. After confirming that Bob was referring to Guest Supply, Manny related to Bob that his brother in-law in Ohio was one of the largest shareholders. Bob wanted to speak with me ASAP and that was the reason for Manny's unusual message on my answering machine that day.

This chance connection between my brother in–law Manny and Bob Shapiro turned out to be absolutely crucial to my attempts to do whatever was necessary to bring about a favorable or, at the least, an acceptable outcome to what had turned into a very difficult situation.

The next morning, I sent the family out for breakfast while I made the call to Shapiro. When they returned, I was still on the phone. Bob loved to talk and we ended up spending more than an hour on the phone every morning for the next five months!

It was very difficult to have a conversation with Bob. He had three phones in his office and often would conduct simultaneous conversations on all three lines at the same time! Another frustration was Bob's habit of constantly going off on tangents during our conversations. Bob was extremely intelligent which I think was part of the problem. His mind was racing in so many different directions that he kept switching gears in the middle of sentences.

Also, Bob would often talk in parables, many of which I was unable to understand. My head was usually spinning after our conversations and even though we may have just spent ninety minutes on the phone, I frequently had no idea what we talked about. I doubt he did either.

I really liked Bob, despite his numerous idiosyncrasies, and I think the feeling was mutual. Of course, it really didn't matter whether I liked him or not. Shapiro had the potential to be a huge influence on how this fiasco would turn out and I was determined to do whatever was necessary, vis-à-vis my relationship with him, to maximize the value of my investment.

The most direct way Shapiro could help was to buy the stock. The stock was in freefall and within days following our initial conversation, he was able to buy a large block of 258,500 shares from a desperate institutional holder that panicked as the price kept dropping. Bob paid $8 5/8; the low for the year.

Because of that one huge purchase at $8 5/8, Bob was viewed as our savior by many of us. The stock price at that time appeared to have no bottom. Any further decline would have triggered additional margin selling pressure and I for one would have been toast. I could foresee being forced to sell my entire position at $4, which wouldn't have generated enough proceeds to cover my margin debt. I am sure several others were in the same boat.

Even if Bob had never bought another share after that, we still would have been extremely grateful that he stepped in and saved us. Obviously, his motivation was to make money for himself and I don't think he ever knew how dire the situation was for many of us at that point.

One of my first tasks once I returned from vacation was to figure out as much as I could about Shapiro from Manny, SEC filings, the internet or any other source I could uncover. I learned from Manny that Shapiro was part of a wealthy Jewish family from Chicago. He thought they had started out in the mink business which somehow morphed into a mink oil business or maybe vice versa. I have no idea what you do with mink oil but Manny thought that Bob's Emlin skin care products used mink oil as one of the main ingredients. Manny was very fuzzy on the details and I suppose past history really didn't matter. I wanted to know how wealthy they were now in regards to their capability of buying a $150 million company.

One thing that concerned me during my conversations with Bob was his reference to several other companies he had wanted to buy but, for one reason or another, his plans never came to fruition. I was concerned that Bob might be a nut case just blowing smoke.

Another interesting sidelight I learned from Manny was that Bob would occasionally mention his family's close relationship with the Pritzker family, another wealthy Jewish family, also from Chicago. Wealthy is really not the right word to describe the Pritzker family as they are one of the richest families in America with Forbes pegging the family's net worth at about $5 billion back in the late 90's. The Pritzker connection would help explain Emlin's Hyatt contract as the Pritzker's owned the Hyatt Hotel chain. Besides Hyatt, the Pritzkers controlled a privately held conglomerate called Marmon Holdings. Marmon owned 60 different businesses at the time, with estimated revenues of nearly $6 billion. Marmon sounded like a perfect home for Guest Supply except for one thing; I doubt that the Hiltons and Marriot's of the world would want to buy their hotel amenities from the owners of Hyatt.

Some of the best information on the Shapiro's came from my discovery in the SEC filings of a small Indianapolis property & casualty insurance company called Baldwin & Lyons. The board of directors sounded like a Shapiro family tree. Four of the nine directors were Shapiro's. There was Nathan who owned a broker-dealer in Chicago by the name of SF Investments. Norton Shapiro was retired from National Superior Fur Dressing & Dyeing Co. I guess Manny was right about the mink business. And of course Bob was listed also. Not listed as a director but included in the filing as a large shareholder was Lester Shapiro. It turns out that Lester, well into his 80's, was the father of Robert, Nathan and Norton.

The Shapiro family owned about one million shares of Baldwin stock at the time, worth about $22 million. A nice sum but certainly not the kind of number that would make you think they could swallow a $200 million company. There also was a Bahamian Trust company listed as owner of 525,000 shares. Upon reading the footnotes, I discovered that this trust was one of the Pritzker family trusts; more evidence of the connection between the two families.

I never was able to pin down the Shapiro Family's net worth. I always hoped it was a big number but I never knew for sure. I desperately wanted this new player in the game to be a home run hitter, not a utility infielder!

As I shared my Shapiro dealings with Dick Sampson, Tom Day and others, there enthusiasm was hard to contain. Especially Tom Day; he was convinced Shapiro was our white knight that would save the day. He was absolutely convinced that the Shapiro's intended to make a tender offer for 100% of Guest Supply.

It didn't help to contain his optimism when he told me he got a call from a 60 year old female client of his from Alabama of all places. She told him that she was a sorority sister of Bob Shapiro's wife 40 years ago and they still talked occasionally. She claimed that she was told by Bob's wife that Bob was going to take over Guest Supply. To this day, I have no idea whether this far fetched story was true or not, but Tom Day still stands by its veracity.

We were all so desperate for Shapiro to be the answer to our prayers that we always put a favorable spin on information or conversations while conveniently omitting things that would tend to throw water on our optimism. For example, I certainly never shared my doubts with anyone about the Shapiro's wealth. As far as anyone was concerned, Bob Shapiro may as well have been Bill Gates.

Word of Shapiro's involvement spread like wildfire among the troops. His involvement added tremendous credibility to the investment thesis regarding Guest Supply. Just as confidence in our own investment acumen was at a low, here were wealthy, experienced investors buying the stock. Additionally they were actually in the hotel amenity business through Bob's Hyatt contract and they had taken control of a public company before, with their holdings in Baldwin & Lyons.

In short, the Shapiro's purchase meant that maybe we all weren't idiots after all. The concrete result of Shapiro's involvement, in the short run, was a steady recovery of the stock price to the $15 area over the next several months.

We had survived the April 1997 inventory debacle but any remaining confidence we had in Cliff Stanley was rapidly eroding.

After three or four weeks of my daily morning phone calls with Bob Shapiro, covering every aspect of Guest Supply and its business, Bob asked me to come to Chicago to "meet his brothers." I was convinced this was D-Day. I envisioned being taken out on Lake Michigan on the family's sail boat where they would lay out their plans to take control of Guest Supply and determine what role the large holders such as me, Sampson, Day & Emoff would play. After all, nobody could get control of Guest Supply without our support or participation; we owned too much stock.

So on July 7th, 1997, I headed to the Windy City with big expectations. I was nervous and concerned that I might say something to screw things up. Bob picked me up at Midway airport in his five year old Oldsmobile. Manny had warned me not to be surprised by Bob's choice of transportation. No Mercedes or Jaguar for Bob. Not even a Cadillac! I wonder what Bill Gates drives.

I got my first letdown when Bob outlined the plans for the day. No sailboat on Lake Michigan, but he did take me to a very fancy downtown Chicago businessman's club for lunch. We were joined for lunch by Bob's older brother Nathan and Nathan's son Steven. Nathan and Steven worked together in their own brokerage operation called SF Investments. At lunch, Steven mentioned that he had heard that Marietta, Guest's largest competitor, was interested in buying Guest. That's the first I had ever heard mention of any interest by Marietta. I got the sense that the question was pre-planned just to gauge my reaction to it. I felt that maybe there was some connection between Marietta and the Shapiro's.

After lunch, the plan was to go to the SF conference room. I never did meet Norton or their father Lester.

As the day wore on, I gradually realized my trip was not about the Shapiro's plans to take control of Guest. It seems as enthusiastic as Bob was about the Guest opportunity, Nathan was the opposite. Although Bob never said so, it became apparent that he wanted me there to convince Nathan of the merits of owning Guest Supply.

Whatever the level of the Shapiro's family's wealth, it was obvious that Bob didn't have the wherewithal to go it alone. No further investment in Guest Supply would be made unless the entire family was on board.

Nathan Shapiro was as tough as nails. He challenged everything. I felt I was on trial. I did everything I could to convince him that Guest would be a $30 stock within two years and now was their opportunity, with everyone so negative.

Nathan was very hard to read. Even if he was buying into what I was telling him, I wouldn't have been able to tell. He spent most of the time thumbing through the new 200 page Guest Supply catalog I had brought with me. He was overwhelmed by the number of different items in the catalog. I had always viewed the large number of SKU's as a good thing; necessary for Guest's strategy of "one stop shopping."

Nathan viewed it much differently. When he looked at the catalog, all he saw was the big cost incurred in stocking all of that inventory, not to mention the logistics of keeping track of everything. Then he would launch into a tirade about the huge costs of stocking sixteen distinct distribution centers all over the country. He wondered how much was spent just to move inventory from one center to another as some centers would run out of an item while another had an excess.

I had never given the issue much thought and even if I had, this type of issue was way beyond my capability to get a handle on. The closest I had come to questioning this strategy was asking Cliff why he needed three distribution centers in Ohio. His answer was they were a holdover from the Company's 1987 purchase of Breckenridge. He claimed that the extra costs incurred were less than the cost to close down the redundant centers. Sort of like his explanation for keeping the antiquated and inefficient plant; the rent was so low he couldn't afford to move. I had naively accepted many of Stanley's explanations over the years, when things were going well, but now, Nathan Shapiro's concerns really gave me pause.

I was somewhat depressed on the flight home compared to the euphoria I felt that morning. I wasn't very confident that the Shapiro's would be buying any more stock but they did have that 258,000 share block, not an insignificant amount. Even if they didn't buy any more, they would have a hard time unloading so much stock, so I felt they were in for the long haul, just like the rest of us.

After I returned to Columbus, the daily calls from Bob continued. He felt that the meeting in Chicago went well and his brother Nathan, while not totally convinced, had given the okay for the family to continue to buy more shares.

8

A Declaration of War

The two strongest quarters for Guest Supply were typically the June and September quarters due to the seasonality of the hotel business. Occupancy rates were much higher in the summer travel season which created strong demand for the Company's products.

As the June 1997 earnings release approached, many of the large investors, including myself, were on edge. We wondered whether all the problems were behind the Company, resulting in great earnings, or was there another cockroach about to appear out of nowhere? Unfortunately, we were now conditioned to expect the worst, unlike the great optimism we had had in prior years. Instead of looking forward to the next earnings release, we became extremely anxious as the date approached; always looking for some clue in something Cliff had said that might give us an insight into how the quarter had gone.

The June 1997 quarter would come in at $.23, three cents better than the prior year but below analyst estimates for the sixth time in the last seven quarters. Sales increased 9.8%, not terrible but certainly not the kind of double digit growth that excited investors. At least there was no big write-off or order deferral. It was the kind of number that would keep the stock in the mid to low teens; no need, for the time being, to worry about a $7 stock and margin calls.

As the summer wore on, I continued to have discussions with Cliff about a board seat. The discussions went nowhere with Cliff feeling very threatened by the whole issue. I think he felt somewhat conflicted about our board seat request. On the one hand, I feel he really empathized with our situation and realized the tremendous pressure we were under from our investors. I also believe that, deep down, he felt somewhat responsible. On the other hand, he saw the board seat request as a personal attack on his leadership of the Company by a bunch of guys that, in his view, would be of no value to the Board.

I had a list on my desk with ten to fifteen names on it. While it was difficult to verify the numbers, this group of names probably controlled over half of the outstanding shares of Guest Supply. I simply felt that there should be at least one board member representing these outside shareholders. Of course the Company's position was that the current Board *did* represent the outside shareholders and therefore there was no need to add anyone new.

My relationship with Cliff Stanley, at this point, was still good. Despite all of the missteps, I continued to believe Guest would eventually realize its great potential and that Cliff Stanley was still capable of getting the Company there or as Gordy would say, taking us from point B to point C.

All we wanted was one board seat. We owned all of this stock and we had stuck with our investment through all of the difficult times. We had way too much stock to ever even think of selling any size at a decent price. The trading volume was too low and a large sale, even if we could find a buyer, would kill the stock price. My feeling was that as long as we were stuck with this investment for the long haul, we should have representation on the Board.

Stanley had two choices; he could continue to stonewall us and thereby create an adversarial relationship with his largest shareholders, who represented over half of the stock, or he could have given one board seat to one of these outside shareholders and by so doing, go a long way towards ensuring the continued support of the outside shareholders.

Stanley made the wrong choice. I certainly wasn't privy to any of their discussions, but I have no doubt that Tom Haythe, Guests' general counsel and long time board member, had a big role in this regrettable decision. After all, Stanley had told me and Dick in late April that he would get us on the Board. That most likely was before he had a chance to broach the subject with Haythe. Of course Haythe's law firm would ultimately be the biggest beneficiary of this decision, as it would generate very substantial legal fees for his firm over the next four years.

I wonder if Cliff ever realized that Haythe's advice could possibly be motivated by something other than maximizing the value for "all" of Guest Supply's shareholders. The decision to fight us became even more difficult to swallow as we began to realize the absurdity of the Company paying legal fees to Haythe so he could keep us off the Board when we owned such a large part of the Company. In essence, the Company was using what we felt was our money to pay Haythe to fight us. It's like taking money out of your pocket and giving it to someone so they can pay their lawyer to sue you!

By mid August, I had had enough. The SEC Form 13G that I had filed at the end of 1996, showing my 8.6% stake in the Company, was adequate for *"passive investors owning more than 5% which was acquired in the normal course of busi-*

ness." Well, I was no longer a "passive investor." It was time to change my filing to a 13D.

A 13D filing can be used as a sort of "declaration of war." The filing has a section that allows you to state your intentions regarding board seats or your thoughts regarding the adequacy of current management, etc. I wasn't sure what language I should use in the filing and I certainly wasn't going to hire some high priced securities lawyer for $5,000 minimum.

I spent about twenty minutes searching various 13D filings on the SEC's electronic filing web site. It didn't take long to find an aggressively worded 13D filing from some money manager that was hacked off at some company I had never heard of. All I did was use the copy and paste function, make a few minor changes and I had my own 13D. Below is an excerpt representing the crux of my filing:

Item 4. PURPOSE OF TRANSACTION

The Reporting Person acquired and continues to hold the shares of stock reported herein for investment purposes. Consistent with such purpose, the Reporting Person has had, and expects to continue to have, discussions with management and other shareholders of the Issuer concerning various operational and financial aspects of the Issuer's business. These discussions will and have included plans and proposals concerning changing the size and composition of the Issuer's board of directors with the goal of obtaining adequate representation for long-term substantial shareholders. The Reporting person may also have discussions with management, directors and other shareholders of the Issuer concerning various ways of maximizing long-term shareholder value.

The filing served several purposes besides showing that my position continued to increase and was now up to 536,637 shares or 8.7% of the Company. While it didn't promise a proxy fight for board seats, it certainly indicated that I wasn't going to go away quietly. Since these filings were public, it served to galvanize the shareholder base, most of whom felt helpless to do anything that might help maximize their investment. Besides the expected calls of support from people like Dick, Tom, Todd, Brad, Bob Shapiro, etc., I also heard from several large shareholders that I had never spoken to before. All were pleased that someone was finally taking some action.

I would later learn that my filing also caused the Board, at the direction of Tom Haythe, to go into full battle mode. The Company already had had in place two of the most commonly used corporate defense mechanisms; a poison pill and a classified board. A classified board meant that only two of the six directors were up for re-election each year. This makes it almost impossible to ever get control of a company's board through a proxy fight.

Now they decided to give golden parachutes to the top management and to Tom Haythe. This is not a misprint! They gave a golden parachute, which pays an exorbitant cash bonus if there is any change of control, to the outside general counsel. I had never seen a golden parachute given to anyone other than a corporation's senior management and I doubt I will ever again see such an outrage as long as I live. We didn't know it then but 3 1/2 years later, this gluttonous action would come within an eyelash of causing irreparable harm to the shareholders of Guest Supply.

All of this was a total overreaction. All we wanted was one board seat but the more the Company fought it, the more I started to think that, maybe, there was some reason I was unaware of which was causing them to be so defensive. On the other hand, all of these corporate actions generated substantial legal fees for Haythe and he was the guy recommending these actions. I couldn't understand at the time why the rest of the Board didn't put a stop to Haythe's ridiculous antics but it would become much clearer to me as I would get to know the other Board members over the next two years.

The Board's paranoia certainly wasn't eased by the mid-November 13D filing from the Shapiro family. Bob had told me they were going to continue to add to their position after that initial block back in June. The filing showed 365,500 shares or a 5.9% stake in the Company. Two weeks later, they would amend their filing to show they had increased their stake to 8%. Most of the additional stock was purchased in the $13-$15 range; a lot higher than that initial block in June at $8 5/8.

There is no doubt in my mind that if Bob had laid low and never called me, he would have been able to buy all of these additional shares at much lower prices. All of the hype that was generated when I let it be well known they were buying stock definitely made it harder and more expensive to buy shares. My guess is that Bob Shapiro's enthusiasm, as evidenced by his daily calls to me, probably cost his family over $1 million!

9

The Battle Begins

My first action after filing my 13D was to submit shareholder proposals to the Company for inclusion in the proxy materials sent to shareholders ahead of the next annual shareholder meeting. The deadline for submission was September 19, 1997 so I didn't have much time. While seemingly a simple process, the SEC rules regarding shareholder proposals are somewhat technical. If the proposal conflicts with any of the numerous SEC guidelines, a company can just refuse to include it in the proxy.

Once again, I was confronted with the choice of spending tons of money and engaging a securities attorney or figuring it out on my own. I decided to finally put to use the law degree I had earned nineteen years earlier. The Rose Capital office in the basement of my home was transformed overnight into a full fledged one-man securities law practice on behalf of the shareholders of Guest Supply. I purchased two 1,000 page legal books; Meetings of Stockholders by Balotti, Finkelstein & Williams and Aranow & Einhorn on Proxy Contests for Corporate Control. I was prepared to do battle with Haythe's big Park Avenue law firm in New York City. Professor Shipman at Ohio State would have been proud of me!

I certainly knew that submitting shareholder proposals were unlikely to have any immediate impact. However, they did allow us to publicly air our numerous grievances with the Company's corporate governance. My intent was to constantly keep pressure on the Board to force them to start taking actions that would benefit the outside shareholders that had real money at stake, not just the insiders that were given an outrageous number of options and rarely actually bought any stock. These actions could be anything from instituting a simple share repurchase plan to selling the Company.

Here is my initial list of the nine potential shareholder proposal topics I was considering:

1. Expand the size of the Board.

2. Restrict future options grants.

3. Re-format income statement to show hotel & contact manufacturing separately.

4. Require share buyback plan.

5. Prohibit re-pricing or extension of existing options.

6. Rescind the poison pill.

7. Require all offers to buy the Company be disclosed to shareholders.

8. Eliminate staggered election of Directors.

Some of these issues go back to the late 80's. As long as the Company's performance was adequate, we let these issues slide or maybe sent a polite letter to the Board. That approach wouldn't do anymore. Besides, the polite letters had very minor impact, if any at all. Once again, if the Company had made any effort to satisfy some of our minor corporate governance concerns, I doubt I would have been firing off shareholder proposals or demanding Board seats.

After researching the shareholder proposal rules in depth, I realized several of the proposals would easily be rejected by the Company. Those that addressed issues solely in the purview of the Board were not allowed. Others could only be phrased as recommendations. Those that required a change in the Company's corporate charter required an 80% vote, an impossible hurdle.

The end result was that four proposals were submitted. Each shareholder can only submit one proposal so I had to get three other shareholders to each send one to the Company. Brad Dolgin, Tom Day, and one of Todd Emoff's clients volunteered. I faxed them each a rough draft and they took it from there. Below are excerpts from the proposal I submitted as well as the Company's opposing statement.

SHAREHOLDER PROPOSAL

RESOLVED: That the Board of Directors increase the size of the board from six to eight and fill these newly created vacancies with representatives of long term shareholders.

Supporting Statement:

The proponent believes that passage of this proposal is necessary to ensure that corporate decisions are made with input from long-term substantial shareholders and with the best interests of shareholders as the highest priority.

THE BOARD OF DIRECTORS RECOMMENDS A VOTE AGAINST **THIS PROPOSAL**

The Board of Directors believes the proposal is inconsistent with the principle that all Directors should represent and act in the interests of *all* shareholders, regardless of how long they have owned their stock. In addition, the requirement that new Directors be representatives of the Company's long—term shareholders could exclude highly—qualified candidates to the detriment of the Company and its shareholders.

The Board believes that the present composition of the Board ensures that the Company is managed in the interests of all shareholders. Only two of the six Directors are employees of the Company, while the four outside Directors bring to the Board decades of independent business and professional experience. Collectively, the Directors own substantial amounts of the Company's stock, as well as options and warrants to acquire stock, which motivates them to act in the interests of shareholders.

The Board remains open to the possibility of adding Directors who would bring particular expertise to the Company. Arbitrarily increasing the size of the Board, however, without regard to such expertise, would make corporate governance more cumbersome and expensive, without any benefit to the Company or its shareholders.

The Board of Directors therefore recommends that shareholders vote AGAINST this proposal.

I hit the roof when I read the language in the opposing statement which stated that the Directors owned substantial amounts of stock and I immediately fired off the following letter to the Company and the SEC:

> I am in receipt of Guest Supply's response to my shareholder proposal concerning adding two directors to the Company's Board. In the opposing statement it is stated "Collectively, the directors own substantial amounts of the Company's stock." I must ask that you remove this part of the statement since it is not a truthful statement and is materially misleading.
>
> In reality, members of the Board own only 1.45% of the outstanding common stock of Guest Supply. No reasonable person would conclude that

1.45% is a "substantial" amount for a small Company such as Guest Supply. Reality would dictate that you change this phrase to "negligible amounts of the Company's stock." In fact, over the last two years, members of the Board have collectively been **net sellers** of the Company stock.

In your response you further state that options positions of the Directors are sufficient to motivate Directors to act in the interests of shareholders. It is apparent that management lacks understanding of the difference between holding options and holding shares. Optionees have no possibility of monetary loss, all they can lose is the potential profit that good results would produce. Shareholders can lose their entire investment. Since optionees do not have their capital invested in the Company's stock, they are able to make alternative uses of that capital which actual shareholders cannot. If management of this Company does understand the difference between these two types of interests, they obviously are choosing to disregard the interests of shareholders in favor of the option holders. That is why this issue is coming to a vote to begin with. That is why this proposal is going to pass overwhelmingly. If the Directors really owned a "substantial amount of the Company's stock" management would have a chance to win the vote. They do not have such stock. I personally own more than twice the amount of shares than all officers and directors combined. I have difficulty fathoming the fact that management is even fighting a proposal to give large long-time shareholders a minority voice on the Board.

In the interests of accuracy, fairness, truth, and legality, the claim that Directors of Guest Supply own "substantial amounts of the Company stock" should be removed from the proxy materials.

The following is the second proposal, submitted by Brad, regarding future options grants:

SHAREHOLDER PROPOSAL

RESOLVED: To amend Guest Supply Inc.'s option and warrant plans to require all future grants to be contingent on achievement of specific corporate profitability levels and share price targets; with such profitability levels and share price targets to be disclosed to shareholders.

Supporting Statement:

This proposal is designed to further align the interests of management with the interests of long term shareholders. Granting greater amounts of stock options for higher levels of incremental financial performance is becoming a more common *system* of executive compensation. This type of system greatly reduces the apparent divergence of interests between shareholders and management that occurs when management benefits financially if the price of the company's stock stays low in the short and intermediate term, thus resulting in a lower exercise price for newly granted stock options.

THE BOARD OF DIRECTORS RECOMMENDS A VOTE AGAINST THIS PROPOSAL

This proposal could trigger highly adverse accounting consequences for the Company. If options or warrants were contingent on the achievement of profitability or stock price targets, the Company would have to record as a compensation expense the difference between the exercise price of the option or warrant shares and the market price of those shares on the date the targets were met. That expense would, of course, reduce reported earnings, and the prospect of such a reduction would tend to have a negative effect on the price of the Company's stock. In contrast, it is the Company's policy not to issue options and warrants that require recognition of any compensation expense.

Furthermore, the Board of Directors believes that this proposal is not needed to accomplish the proponent's stated purpose. Options and warrants under the Company's existing plans are inherently performance based, since they are granted at the prevailing market price. If the stock price does not increase after the date of grant, the options or warrants have no value. Thus, the Company's existing options and warrants align the interests of management with the interests of shareholders, and do not create any financial benefit to the grantees if the price of the Company's stock remains at the levels prevailing on the date of grant.

Finally, options and warrants are an important element in the compensation of executives and other valued employees. Adding conditions to the Company's options and warrants that are not customary would put the Company at a competitive disadvantage in attracting and retaining talented personnel.

The Board of Directors therefore recommends that shareholders vote AGAINST this proposal.

The proposal concerning disclosure of offers to acquire the Company was submitted by Todd Emoff's client. This proposal was based on our suspicions that Guest Supply may have been approached by its main competitor, Marietta Corp., and possibly the Shapiro's about a possible acquisition. Here is that proposal:

SHAREHOLDER PROPOSAL

RESOLVED: To recommend that the management of Guest Supply, Inc. disclose to shareholders any future offers to acquire the Company and submit such offers for shareholder consideration and advisory vote.

Supporting Statement:

This proposal, while not requiring the Board to approve of any transaction, is designed to ensure that shareholders receive all information pertaining to their ownership interest in the Company. The proposal also will allow the Board of Directors to be apprised of the views of shareholders concerning any such offers.

THE BOARD OF DIRECTORS RECOMMENDS A VOTE AGAINST THIS PROPOSAL

The Board of Directors believes that this proposal would seriously interfere with its obligation and ability properly to consider transactions covered by the proposal. Premature and incomplete disclosure, which could result from adoption of the proposal, would impair the Board's ability to pursue offers or expressions of interest that appear to be in the best interests of the Company and its shareholders. Indeed, since potential purchasers often seek to initiate negotiations on a confidential basis, the Board believes that this proposal, if adopted, could have the effect of discouraging offers for the Company.

The Board also believes that the proposal is so broadly worded that it would create uncertainty as to the Directors' obligations when considering possible transactions, particularly in determining whether informal or exploratory bids might be deemed "offers." The Board has been advised by counsel that the proposal would raise potential conflicts with federal law regarding disclosure of material information and with New York Stock Exchange rules regarding the confidentiality of merger or acquisition discussions.

Finally, premature disclosure could have a disruptive effect on the market for the Company's stock, potentially creating artificial and erratic price movements. It could also create uncertainty among the Company's customers, suppliers and employees, leading to instability in relationships with these important constituencies. Both results would be detrimental to the company and its shareholders.

The Board of Directors therefore recommends that shareholders vote against this proposal.

The final proposal concerned re-pricing and/or extending the expiration date of options and was submitted by Tom Day:

SHAREHOLDER PROPOSAL

RESOLVED: To require shareholder approval of any change in the terms of any options or warrants granted to officers, employees or directors, including in the exercise price or expiration date.

Supporting Statement:

While the proponent strongly supports the reasonable use of incentive stock options for key employees, this proposal seeks to prevent management from changing the terms of previously granted options because of the failure of the company over the last two years to meet reasonable profitability objectives which has resulted in a substantial decline in the share price of the Company's stock. It should also be noted that the Company has in the past both extended the expiration date and reduced the exercise price (from $8 to $3) of previously granted options.

THE BOARD OF DIRECTORS RECOMMENDS A VOTE A3AINST THIS PROPOSAL

This sweeping proposal would restrict the Board's ability to make any change in the terms of outstanding options or warrants. If adopted, it would require shareholder approval even of routine amendments designed to conform the Company's option and warrant plans to changing legal and tax requirements.

The Board believes that in order to provide realistic compensation packages for employees and management, it must retain discretion to modify the price and expiration terms of options and warrants. Unusual business and economic circumstances, over which employees have no control, may require such modifications to preserve the incentive function of options and warrants. The Board has exercised its discretion to modify option and warrant terms sparingly. It has not repriced or extended the terms of any options or warrants since April 1990 and February 1991, when it authorized certain key employees and Directors to exchange options exercisable at $7.75 per share for options or warrants exercisable at $4.75 per share, and extended the expiration date of certain warrants from 1993 to 1998. Those actions were taken at a time when the Company, following a change in senior management, was experiencing serious financial difficulties. They were intended to provide a non—cash incentive to key employees and Directors during a period of great uncertainty that required extraordinary commitment, and the Board believes they accomplished that objective.

The Board has not recently considered and does not presently intend to make any changes in the *price* or expiration terms of any existing options or warrants.

The Board of Directors therefore recommends that shareholders vote AGAINST this proposal.

In response to his proposal, Tom Day received a letter from the Company suggesting that he was part of my "13D group" and that he should discuss the matter with his firm's SEC compliance department. Needless to say, this scared the heck out of Tom Day. He was all for fighting with Stanley & Haythe but not if it meant he could lose his job.

I had been anticipating that Haythe would attempt to use the 13D group rules to derail our efforts. The 13D group rules basically say that all shareholders that are part of a group that collectively own more than 5% of a company constitute a 13D group and must file a single Form 13D which discloses all members of the group. The SEC has no problem with shareholders joining together as a group as long as it's disclosed. The problem is figuring out what constitutes a "group."

The SEC defines a group as "*two or more persons agreeing to act together for the purpose of acquiring, holding, voting or disposing of equity securities of an issuer.*" Without getting into all of the various legal interpretations, I felt that we were not a group because we had no agreements concerning buying or selling shares, voting or taking any other actions against the Company.

I am convinced that Haythe knew that we weren't a 13D group but he felt that there was just enough doubt that it might scare us away, which was his main intent. What concerned me was the real possibility that he still might pursue the issue with the SEC, which would have been a time consuming and expensive process for me to fight. I don't think I could have handled that from my basement Rose Capital office.

I figured the best way to counteract his threat was to respond aggressively. Within a week, I had drafted the following letter for Tom's signature addressed to Paul Xenis, Guest Supply's CFO and Corporate Secretary:

October 17, 1997

Mr. Paul Xenis
Guest Supply, Inc.
P.O. Box 902
Monmouth Junction, NJ 08852-0902

Dear Mr. Xenis,

I received your letter regarding my shareholder proposal to require shareholder approval of any change in option terms. In the letter you ask if I am a member of a "13D group." If I were a member of a "13D group", I would have filed as such. I'll tell you what "group" I am in. I am in a "group" called GUEST SUPPLY SHAREHOLDERS. This is the group that owns the Company.

I.don't have to be in a "13D group" to be extremely concerned about the events (or lack thereof) over the last two years:

1) Earnings estimates missed 6 out of last 7 Qtrs.

2) $2 million inventory write-off due to mismanagement.

3) 3 trading halts in the Company's stock

4) Continual order deferrals and pricing adjustments with a large contract pkg. customer. The overdependence on a single customer has been obvious for over 2 years, yet we are approaching Nov, 1997 and we are more dependent than ever on this customer, you have failed to execute a long term agreement with this customer, and have not announced any new contract pkg. customers.

5) Failure to execute a share re-purchase program when the decline to $8 1/8 created an obvious opportunity to reduce shares outstanding and increase EPS.

6) Refusal to expand the Board to allow for greater shareholder representation.

Sincerely,

Thomas E. Day

There was no response to the letter. I am sure Haythe and Stanley were too embarrassed after seeing their failures laid out in black & white.

10

Deep Throat & the Thanksgiving Ambush

When the Shapiro's filed their initial form 13D in November of 1997, the daily phone calls from Bob mysteriously stopped. I didn't think much of it at first. I though that maybe, he was traveling out of the country and I would hear from him again in a week or so. After about ten days, I decided to call him. He took the call and informed me that his attorney instructed him to no longer communicate with me. He was concerned that our constant communication would be evidence that we were a "13D group."

I felt that it took a lot more than telephone conversations to establish a 13D group but Bob wasn't interested in my legal analysis. I know it was difficult for him to not call me because he loved to go on and on about what he perceived as gross mismanagement by Stanley. And of course he was preaching to the choir when he spoke to me about Stanley at that point.

My goal was to reinforce with Bob our belief in the tremendous earnings power of Guest Supply, if only it was run correctly. I thought that this earnings potential would motivate him, at the least, to keep buying additional shares and hopefully make an offer to buy the entire Company.

Of course, I tried to put a positive spin on Bob's cessation of communication. Why else would he be worried about the 13D group rules unless he planned on going after the Company and wanted to make sure Haythe couldn't derail his efforts on a technicality?

This positive spin was typical of how many of us treated every little bit of information concerning Guest. The hope was that the hype would keep anyone from selling their stock and maybe even create some additional buying. We all knew the game but nobody was better at it than Tom Day. If it had been discovered that Guest Supply's shampoo was causing cancer, Tom Day would have found a way to turn it into a positive for the stock!

Although Bob stopped calling me, he would occasionally and reluctantly take my call but the conversations were fairly short. I was like a drug dealer offering drugs to an addict who was trying to kick the habit.

After a few weeks of this cat and mouse game with Bob, I received a call from my brother in-law Manny in Atlanta. Manny was the one responsible for making the original connection between me and Bob Shapiro. He told me that Bob had called him and suggested that we use Manny as a liaison between us. When I had some information or question for Bob, I would call Manny who would pass it along to Bob and vice versa. From that point on, Manny was referred to by the Watergate era moniker of "Deep Throat." Whenever I spoke to Dick, Todd or Tom about any contact with the Shapiro's, they would always ask if I had spoken to Deep Throat lately.

Dick Sampson had a unique position in the Guest Supply saga. Not only was he responsible, in one way or another, for getting most of the large shareholders involved initially, he also had an interesting relationship with Cliff Stanley. When Dick first got involved with Guest in the late 80's, Cliff had just been named CEO and the excessive options grants were soon to follow. Cliff saw the huge potential financial upside for himself if he could turn around the Company *and* get the stock to trade at a high multiple to earnings. The landscape is littered with solidly growing micro-cap companies that never get discovered by investors and therefore trade at low multiples to their earnings. Cliff saw Dick Sampson as just the guy to get the story out. Stanley bought into Dick's supply and demand theory which said the more demand you create for a stock, the higher the price will be. The unspoken arrangement was that, in return for Dick becoming a crusader for the Guest Supply story, he would have unprecedented access to Cliff and every bit of information related to the Company.

Dick was very well suited to his unofficial role. He had a low key manner and was fairly unemotional, in contrast to many of the other large shareholders including myself. The only problem was that when things really got bad, as they had in 1996 & 1997, Dick would become depressed and withdrawn for weeks and sometimes months at a time. During these times, not only did he stop calling us, but he wouldn't return any messages we would leave for him. I think he must have felt totally helpless in the face of the incredible problems the Company was having. Because of his close relationship with Cliff Stanley, many of us looked to Dick for answers, and when he didn't have any he just withdrew himself from the whole mess. Many of us empathized with what he was going through personally, but we were suffering too and we felt he was abandoning us when we needed him the most.

Whenever I wanted Cliff Stanley to be aware of something, all I had to do was mention it to Dick and I could be assured that the information would get to Stanley within a day or two. Such was the case in November 1997 when I wanted Cliff to know that I intended to submit nominations for the two Board seats up for reelection at the next annual shareholders meeting. I figured that warning Cliff of what was coming might get him to realize I was serious and hopefully prompt him to give us the Board seats without a fight. I knew it was a long shot but I didn't see much downside in it. At that point, I had no idea what was involved but I had plenty of time to figure that out before the January 5th deadline for submitting Board nominations to the Company.

As I was loading up the car the afternoon before Thanksgiving, I was looking forward to a few days when I could just forget about Guest Supply. We were headed to Shawnee State Park lodge in Southern Ohio for our annual tradition of spending Thanksgiving with my wife's large extended family.

It was around 6pm and we were about one hundred miles south of Columbus, about half way to the lodge, when my cell phone rang. I remember wondering how I still had cell service in the middle of nowhere. It was Todd Emoff calling from his office. Only Todd would still be working at 6pm on Thanksgiving Eve!

He told me a news release from Guest Supply had just hit his screen announcing that the annual shareholder meeting date had been set for January 15, 1998. This wouldn't have been unusual except for the fact that the Company's annual meeting had always been in March.

As I was listening to Todd, the reason for moving up the meeting date hit me. The January 5th deadline for submitting Board nominations was based on the Company's charter requiring submissions be made 60 days before the anniversary date of the prior years March 5th meeting date.

By moving the meeting to January 15th, that made the deadline November 15th. I had missed the deadline because they had moved up the meeting date!

I had never been so angry. The worst part was I was stuck out in the woods of Southern Ohio feeling totally helpless until Monday morning when I would be back in the office.

All weekend, I was confused as to why the Company felt it necessary to issue the press release at ten minutes to six on Thanksgiving Eve. When I got back in the office on Monday, I quickly figured out the reason. It seems the SEC rules don't allow a Company to foreclose Board nominations by accelerating the annual meeting date. If a Company does this, a shareholder has a ten day grace period to submit nominations once a company announces the meeting date.

Haythe chose that time to issue the notice for two reasons; first, he hoped no one would ever see it because nobody is in their office at 5:50pm on Thanksgiving Eve. Secondly, if we didn't see it until Monday, five days of the grace period would already be gone, making it more difficult to get the nominations submitted in time.

Obviously, Mr. Haythe didn't count on Todd Emoff working on Thanksgiving Eve, but those of us who know Todd were not surprised.

11

Falling For the Bluff

Tom Haythe's Thanksgiving Eve ploy backfired in a major way for the Company for two reasons. First of all, it enraged most of the large shareholders who got wind of Haythe's antics. Secondly, it ultimately allowed me to get a Board seat that I probably wouldn't have gotten otherwise.

The talk before Thanksgiving of staging a proxy vote to win Board seats was just that, talk. I had no idea how to wage a successful proxy fight. I figured I had plenty of time to research the feasibility of waging and winning a proxy battle during December, well before the assumed filing deadlines. My intent was to scare the Company into negotiating and thereby winning the battle without actually firing a shot.

When I returned to the office after Thanksgiving, I spent two full days pouring over the SEC proxy contest rules and I was very discouraged by the conclusions I reached. Basically, the deck is stacked in favor of the company.

There were several factors that conspired against me. First of all, despite the fact that I had a list on my desk of ten or fifteen names that controlled over 50% of the stock, turning all of those shares into votes would be very difficult and expensive. Most of the stock was held by individual clients of brokers and money managers. I would have to hire a proxy solicitation firm to do numerous mailings and phone calls. I estimated that the cost of hiring the firm plus paying for printing, postage, long distance charges, etc. could easily run to $150,000.

Secondly, there was no way to predict what the legal fees would have been to defend all of the bogus lawsuits that I am sure Haythe would have filed based on the 13D group rules and whatever else he would have dreamed up. I had no doubt it would have been at least another $50,000 in legal fees, maybe even double or triple that amount.

I could have probably raised a war chest from many of the names on my list except for the fact that SEC rules prohibited it, unless we all agreed to jointly file as a 13D group. Filing as a 13D group was impossible based on the fact that many of the large holders worked for the big Wall Street firms which would have quickly vetoed such an attempt. Also, all members of a 13D group would have been required to publicly report all of their holdings as well as any future transactions in Guest Supply stock, something no one wanted to do if they didn't have to.

The deep-pocketed Shapiro's would have been the logical party to take on this whole undertaking but Bob refused to do it. He was 100% in support of my efforts and actually encouraged me to go forward but the rules prohibited him from footing the bill. As far as doing the whole thing himself, the family preferred to stay in the background and let others, meaning me, do their dirty work.

This is when it became clear to me that one of the purposes of Bob's constant phone calls was to use me to do the things they were not comfortable doing themselves. Basically, they were trying to use me as their front man at the same time I was trying to use their large stock purchases and supposed financial stature to threaten the Company. In hindsight, I think the tacit arrangement worked very well, although I was fairly irritated, at the time, when I realized I was being used.

The bottom line was that if I wanted to wage a successful proxy fight, I would have to foot the bill myself, something I couldn't do without selling a big chunk of my stock. Even if I had the cash lying around, I still wouldn't have done it because all we could get was two out of the six Board seats and a minority position on the Board really couldn't force any change. Because of the Company's staggered Board elections, getting a majority was a two or three year process, with most of the costs being repeated each year.

So my threat of a proxy fight was a total bluff, but no one else knew this and, lo and behold, on the Tuesday after Thanksgiving, Dick Sampson called to tell me that the Company wanted to negotiate. My bluff had worked and I'm not even a poker player. It was an easy bluff to make because I really didn't have anything to lose, unlike an actual poker bluff, if the Company had called me on it.

I think what really scared the heck out of the Company, and caused them to panic, was the fortuitous fact that the two Board members that happened to be up for re-election, under the Company's staggered system, were Cliff Stanley and Teri Unsworth, the Company's VP of Marketing. These two were the only Company employees on the Board. For better or for worse, Stanley and Unsworth were absolutely the two key people in the operation of the Company. At a small company like Guest Supply, there simply weren't any other employees that could step in and replace them.

Regardless of what Haythe thought the odds were of us winning a proxy fight, he probably felt he just couldn't take the chance of letting it go that far. The potential embarrassment to Stanley and the Company, as well as the real possibility that the hot-tempered Stanley might resign as CEO in the wake of a defeat were more than Haythe was willing to risk.

Dick Sampson's call to inform me of the Company's desire to negotiate the Board seat issue marked the beginning of a new role for Dick. Now, he was not only Guest Supply's unofficial cheerleader, but he took on the additional role as a buffer between Cliff Stanley and many of the large shareholders, including myself. It was an emotionally charged time and Dick was the only person that had the confidence of both sides.

It was a difficult balancing act for Sampson but he was well suited for the role. He saw it as absolutely crucial given his huge personal stake in the Company. His biggest fear was an all out battle that would cost the Company a tremendous amount of money, let alone the major distraction it would be for Stanley, causing him to lose his primary focus on running the business. Dick did the best he could but there were many times when I wondered if his loyalties lied with Cliff. I am sure Cliff felt the opposite. In hindsight, I think Dick wanted to exert as much pressure on the Company as possible, as long as it didn't distract Stanley or cause an excessive use of Guest's financial resources.

My discussions with Haythe lasted several days and often extended well into the night. He was trying to draw out the process so I wouldn't have any time left under the ten day grace period for submitting Board nominations. I thwarted this tactic by refusing to continue the discussions unless the Company extended the deadline, in writing, for ten days past the end of negotiations, if no agreement was reached.

After Haythe agreed to my demand, the next roadblock was his insistence that all of the large shareholders sign a lock-up agreement in return for giving us one Board seat. The lock-up agreement was intended to prevent any of us from ever supporting or participating in any future proxy contest against the Company.

Maybe I would have possibly considered such a request if it had been made eight months earlier before the situation had turned ugly, but now it was a non-starter. There was no way I was going to give these guys a permanent free pass in return for one lousy Board seat.

This particular issue was resolved by my agreeing to use my best efforts to get all of the other large holders to also sign the agreement. I did send the agreement to Sampson, Shapiro, Day, Dolgin & Emoff but I had no real leverage over them and, of course, no one else signed it. Not even Dick Sampson! Haythe had to know this provision wouldn't hold water. I think it must have been a stab in the dark on his part in an attempt to support his "13D group" allegation. In any event, I used my "best efforts", whatever that means!

Basically, the final agreement gave me a Board seat for at least the next two years. I had to agree not to participate in or support any proxy contest in the future, unless I gave the Company notice ahead of time. The Company also agreed to add a second nominee, mutually agreeable to me and the Board, at next year's annual meeting. I knew we would never "mutually agree" on any potential nominee.

Here is the summary of the eight page agreement that appeared in the proxy materials sent to shareholders by the Company on December 10, 1997:

STOCKHOLDERS AGREEMENT

Upon the mailing of this Proxy Statement, the Company and Barry Igdaloff will become parties to a Stockholders Agreement (the "Stockholders Agreement") pursuant to which Mr. Igdaloff agrees to vote the shares of Common Stock controlled by him for the election of the Company's nominees for director at the Meeting. Additionally, unless Mr. Igdaloff gives a notice to the Company (the "Notice") under certain circumstances, he agrees to vote the shares of Common

Stock controlled by him for the election of the Company's nominees for director at the Annual Meeting of Shareholders held following the end of the Company's 1998 fiscal year (the "1999 Meeting").

The Stockholders Agreement also provides that if the Company's nominees are elected as directors at the Meeting, the Company and the Board of Directors will elect Mr. Igdaloff as a new Class B director promptly following the Meeting and will nominate him for reelection as a Class B director at the 1999 Meeting. In addition, if the Company's nominees are elected as directors at the Meeting, no Notice is given and there shall not have been any solicitation of proxies relating to the Company after the date of the Stockholders Agreement not publicly supported by a resolution of a majority of the current members of the Board of Directors (a "Solicitation"), the Company and the Board of Directors will nominate for election as a director at the 1999 Meeting an individual mutually agreed upon by the President of the Company, a majority of the other members of the Board of Directors and Mr. Igdaloff.

The Stockholders Agreement also provides that (i) until the earlier to occur of the 1999 Meeting or the giving of a Notice, Mr. Igdaloff will not engage in or assist in any Solicitation, (ii) Mr. Igdaloff will not, in any event, nominate any individual for election as a director of the Company or vote for any individual as a director of the Company who is not nominated by a majority of the current members of the Company's Board of Directors (a "Continuing Director Nominee") if the election of such individual (and all other individuals who are not Continuing Director Nominees) would result in less than a majority of the directors of the Company being Continuing Director Nominees and (iii) Mr. Igdaloff will use his best efforts to have other holders of Common Stock execute and deliver the Stockholders Agreement and thereby agree to the provisions thereof applicable to him (other than election as a director of the Company).

Mr. Igdaloff, age 42, has been the principal of Rose Capital, a registered investment advisor, since December 1995. From January 1990 to December 1995, Mr. Igdaloff was a financial advisor with Prudential Securities. As of November 1, 1997, Mr. Igdaloff beneficially owned 536,637 shares of Common Stock, which number includes shares of Common Stock owned by advisory clients of Rose Capital.

12

The Jump on Board

As 1997 was coming to a close, I anxiously awaited the upcoming January 15th annual shareholder meeting. While I was glad the shareholder agreement was concluded and I would soon be joining the Board, it was obvious to me that Haythe and Stanley would do whatever was necessary to protect their little fiefdom. They gave up one Board seat but they had no intention of letting it go any further.

Of course, I hoped that the problems were behind the Company and that the Board would start to immediately take the necessary actions to maximize the value of the shares, but I was not optimistic. In this regard, I started preparing a laundry list of items that I felt should be addressed by the Company.

One of the problems was Cliff Stanley's oft stated view that "if sales kept increasing, sooner or later this would result in a higher valuation for the Company." The problem is the "sooner or later" reference. We had already been in this stock for close to a decade! I think the major shareholders had shown more than enough patience. It was time to either quickly fix the problems or let someone else fix them, either as a result of a management change or possibly selling the entire Company.

One of the ways that I felt I could protect myself against any legal or SEC action initiated by Haythe was to have plenty of documentation of the many legally questionable Company actions that occurred on a regular basis. In December of 1997, I started to keep a journal on my desk that detailed everything that went on, with exact dates and times. Most of these items were examples of selective disclosure of material inside information made to Dick Sampson, but other large shareholders were involved as well.

As December wore on, there was optimism about the next quarterly earnings release in January. The fairly conservative estimate was $.20 vs. the prior years $.17. The December quarter had typically been a slow quarter for the Company due to the seasonality of the hotel business but it had now become very important because of the huge pre-Christmas orders from Bath & Body Works.

Numerous warning signs started to appear regarding the upcoming earnings release. Cliff refused to give the Company's sole research analyst any guidance regarding the quarter. He also stopped returning any investor phone calls. As a result, the stock started to drift lower on fears of yet another earnings debacle, dipping below $12. I was oblivious to the warning signs, as my primary focus that month was my discussions with Haythe regarding Board seats and the shareholder agreement.

As the year ended, I was naively still optimistic about the December quarter earnings. I was also encouraged by a couple of comments Dick Sampson made to me during the month. Haythe had told Dick earlier in the month that he believed the stock was worth $25 and he intended to buy some stock. This would have been a badly needed confidence boost but not surprisingly, he never did follow through with actual purchases.

Cliff Stanley had also told Dick right before Christmas that the hotel distribution business was up 30% for the quarter. I guess despite not returning anyone else's phone calls, he still was in contact with Dick. Another intriguing comment Cliff made to Dick was that there were eight to ten potential "white knights" that would be willing to buy the Company.

In hindsight, it should have been obvious to me that you don't need "white knights" unless you have a problem. At the time, I just took the comment as positive affirmation of my view that Guest Supply's business was a valuable franchise.

About ten days before the January 15th annual shareholder meeting, I received a phone call from Cliff Stanley. He wanted to take me to dinner the night before the meeting. It seemed like his intent was to try to repair our relationship. I guess he was resigned to the fact that I was on the Company's Board for the foreseeable future and he might as well make the best of it. However, I got the sense from his voice that this dinner wasn't his idea and that Haythe had probably strongly suggested he make the call. Stanley was smart enough to realize, especially now, that his fate rested with maintaining the support of Haythe, who basically controlled the Board. After dozens of conversations with Stanley over the last eight years, I could tell something wasn't right.

I decided to use the one on one opportunity over dinner to lay out my list of items that I wanted addressed immediately by the Company. As I met Stanley that night, he seemed tired, nervous and uptight. He really didn't want to be there and it seemed like the whole situation was getting to him. Of course, I had very little empathy for him at that point and I immediately launched into my prepared notes of my take on the current situation.

I told him I was assuming the Company was going to continue its pattern of missing the analyst estimates for not only the just ended December quarter but the next quarter as well due to continuing problems in the contract manufacturing business. I said that these earnings shortfalls will cause many of the major shareholders to throw in the towel and sell their stock because of the manufacturing problems despite the great numbers in the hotel distribution business.

I told him that the Shapiro's would probably come in and soak up all of this stock below $10 and Cliff will wish he still had people like me and Tom Day as shareholders. I explained that he most likely would lose his job as well as control of the Company he had worked so long and hard to build.

Trying to find a "white knight" at that point would be too late. With the stock likely well below $10, he would be lucky to find a buyer at $14, some 40% below the year end price of two years earlier. Besides, the Shapiro's would own so much stock at that point, they could block any offer.

I summarized by telling him that he "simply ran out of time." The shareholders had lost confidence in him and wouldn't be willing to give him another year to try and straighten things out.

Stanley just took it all in and sat there with a blank stare. I don't even know if he really comprehended what I was telling him. I then laid out the following steps that I felt needed to be taken immediately if he was to have any chance of avoiding the fate I had just outlined:

1. Begin an aggressive stock repurchase program after the earnings release.

2. Announce the hiring of an investment banker to "explore strategic alternatives to maximize shareholder value." These are code words for announcing a company is for sale.

3. Break out the hotel results separately on the income statement so the shareholders could see what a great business it is. Guest had always lumped both businesses together because Cliff didn't want customers and competitors to see his margins.

4. Announce a search for a new Chief Operating Officer to run the day to day business with Cliff remaining Chairman.

Regarding this last item, Bob Shapiro had fairly regularly mentioned a close younger business associate of his by the name of Mark Porter. Porter was running a family owned Chicago-based $800 million textile distribution company. He had previously worked for "chainsaw" Al Dunlap, a famous slash and burn corporate turn-around specialist who finally ran out of rabbits to pull out of his hat when he bankrupted Sunbeam.

Bob would tell me that Porter wanted to get out of the family dominated situation he was currently in. He felt there was no real future for him because he wasn't a member of the controlling family. Bob would frequently get Porter on the phone with us whenever he was trying to make a point about some business strategy mistake he felt Guest was making. One of his favorites was his disdain for Guest's three distribution centers in Ohio.

After Bob's lawyers ordered him to stop talking with me, I would occasionally continue to have discussions with Porter. No one ever actually mentioned the possibility that Porter would be the perfect guy to run Guest Supply but it was apparent to all three of us that Porter would be ready, willing and able to step in if it came to that.

One fact that Bob conveniently failed to mention to me and which I would only become aware of several months later was that Mark Porter was Bob Shapiro's son in-law!

I explained to Cliff that these steps I had outlined would be a huge advantage to everybody, including him. The stock price would rise, the shareholders would become optimistic again and therefore willing to give the Company more time to fix its problems and the Shapiro's wouldn't be able to buy up huge blocks of stock at low prices. In essence, these moves would take the pressure off of Cliff and buy him more time.

I told him the alternative was to possibly lose control of the Company and be forced to look for a new job. It didn't matter whether this was justified or not; this was how Wall Street worked. Perception is reality.

Our dinner ended without much comment or reaction from Cliff regarding my suggestions. He was hesitant to share any information with me regarding earnings, future business or other initiatives the Company might be considering. After all, I would not officially be on the Board until the next afternoon and I suspect he felt it would be premature to start discussing inside information with me. This somewhat handcuffed him in responding to my comments.

I had a difficult time sleeping that night in anticipation of the next day's meeting. The shareholders' meeting was scheduled for 10AM at the Princeton, New Jersey Novotel Hotel, where I was staying. It was my custom every time I checked into a hotel, to immediately go into the bathroom and check if Guest Supply was the amenity supplier. It was a win-win proposition for me. If Guest was the supplier, I was pleased because it represented revenue for the Company. If Guest was not the supplier, I took it as a positive because here was potential additional business for the Company. The Novotel did not use Guest Supply products; a strange choice of locations for the Company's annual meeting.

The annual meeting was fairly uneventful. It was attended by ten or fifteen shareholders including Emoff and Day. No Sampson or Shapiro. Most sophisticated corporate shareholders viewed annual meetings as a required legal necessity and rarely worth their time to attend. In fact, this was my first Guest Supply annual shareholder meeting.

One shareholder who always attended was Barry Florescue, the chairman and controlling shareholder of privately held Marietta Corporation. Marietta was Guest Supply's biggest competitor. Barry was a portly man who made it a point to sit front and center, with a little smirk on his face, where Stanley couldn't help having to look right at him as he made his presentation. It made Cliff extremely uncomfortable. The two were bitter enemies and Cliff would constantly bring up examples of what he considered dishonest business practices from Florescue's past.

I suspect Florescue enjoyed immensely Stanley's continuing inability to report consistent profits but I am sure he was also outraged at Guest Supply's aggressive pricing, designed to gain market share at any cost. There was a general consensus in the industry that Guest's strategy was making it difficult, if not impossible, for anyone to earn a decent profit in the hotel amenity business.

I doubt Florescue attended to hear Cliff's presentation; I think he came just because he knew it irritated Stanley.

After the 45 minute shareholder meeting, I needed to check out of the Hotel before heading to the Board meeting at the Company's headquarters, which was about five minutes away. As I was waiting at the front desk, I struck up a conversation with Ed Walsh, one of Guests' Directors. Walsh, in his late 60's and retired, was one of those career Board members. His claim to fame was a very brief stint as CEO of Dial Corporation. He was on several Boards, which in total paid him a very nice income. Guys like Walsh are characterized by their convivial personality and their reluctance to do anything to rock the boat. He owned very little stock but was given 97,500 options by the Company. In Haythe and Stanley's eyes, he was a perfect Board member; absolutely no threat to their authority and his bio looked great in the proxy. To say the least, most shareholders had nothing but disdain for these corporate leeches that, in theory, were supposed to represent the interests of the shareholders!

During my brief conversation with Walsh, I got my first concrete confirmation of another terrible quarter. He was mumbling his frustration with the Company's inability to fix the manufacturing plant problems. Despite Stanley's insistence that most of the problems were behind us, it was now apparent that we weren't out of the woods yet.

When I arrived at the Company headquarters, Cliff asked me to wait in one of the empty offices and someone would come out of the Boardroom to get me after the Board had passed the resolution adding me to the Board. The terms of the shareholder agreement I had negotiated with the Company specifically required the Board to pass this resolution as "*the first order of business.*"

I was left sitting in that office for over an hour! I was livid, to say the least. I was already extremely apprehensive about the prospects of another disastrous earnings announcement as a result of my earlier brief conversation with Walsh. I felt that Haythe and Stanley were intentionally jerking me around. At the very least, I suspected they were plotting how to somehow exclude me from hearing or seeing any confidential Board information.

I will never know for sure what was actually discussed during that hour, but I was able to see the meeting minutes prior to the next Board meeting in April. According to the minutes, that time was spent electing the officers of the Company, as well as setting up all of the various Board committees, such as audit, compensation, nominating, etc.

One committee that was established at that meeting, for the very first time, was an executive committee. This committee's purpose was to be empowered to act, in the place of the Board, in between quarterly Board meetings. They appointed five of the six current Directors to this committee. It was just as I feared. They intended to use this committee to exclude me from discussions and decision making whenever they saw fit!

At the April Board meeting, I threatened to bring legal action if this executive committee ploy wasn't rescinded immediately. I think they were surprised I discovered their outrageous ploy, buried deep in the minutes. They agreed to amend the executive committee resolution so that it would only be used if they were unable to get a quorum for a full board meeting. I knew that the number needed for a quorum of the executive committee plus myself, would result in a quorum for the whole Board, so this amendment effectively stymied their efforts to exclude me. The result was that any ounce of trust I still had left for Haythe and Stanley had gone out the window.

When Haythe finally came out of the meeting, instead of asking me to join the meeting, he came into the small office I had been couped up in, accompanied by Peter Richard, one of the other Board members. He closed the door and made a final attempt to persuade me not to actually join the Board. He explained that I would be restricted from buying or selling stock for myself or my clients, except for short windows after each quarterly earnings release. He stated that even these short windows could be closed if some material corporate item was pending at the time. He also offered to let me sign a confidentiality agreement with the Company, in lieu of joining the Board, which would allow the Company to share inside information with me, as long as I didn't trade on it or disclose it to anyone else.

I had come too far to retreat at this point, so I declined his offer. I told him, as a former attorney and CPA, that I was fully aware of the restrictions that would be placed on me as a result of joining the Board. I guess he had Peter Richard in the room to be a witness to everything that was said. I doubt Haythe thought there was much chance of me deciding to accept his offer and not join the Board, but he probably felt there was no harm in trying.

I finally took my seat in the boardroom, eagerly anticipating a discussion of the myriad of problems facing the Company and, of course, learning at last what the earnings were for the recently ended December quarter. Once again, I was disappointed as I sat there and had to listen to the audit partner from the Company's accounting firm drone on and on about mundane accounting issues. Most of this had very little relevance to Guest Supply but was required to be discussed as part of the year end audit process.

As I glanced around the room, I noticed the other Directors had a nervous and somewhat pensive look on their faces. They also each had a thin package of meeting materials in front of them. I am sure Haythe and Stanley intentionally did not give me this package, intending to delay the inevitable as long as possible. They knew I would not be pleased, to say the least, by what I would read in that package of materials. Finally, as the audit partner droned on, I quietly asked Teri Unsworth, who was seated next to me, if I could see her package. She handed me her package and as I begin to read it, I noticed the other Directors furtively watching me. It was almost as if they were holding their breath, waiting to gauge my reaction to the materials.

Their concern was warranted. I certainly was expecting a small miss in the quarterly earnings but I never anticipated what I saw. The Company was going to report earnings of $.06 versus a conservative estimate of $.20 and the prior years $.17. There was no question the stock would be headed well into single digits again. I wasn't sure whether I could survive the margin calls again. I envisioned being forced to sell my stock with no buyers in sight. If I only got $5 or $6 for it, there would be nothing left after paying off the margin debt. I was sure I would lose a big chunk of my client base as well.

To make matters worse, the five year projection included in the materials showed 2002 earnings of $1.59, a number that many of us thought the Company would reach in 1998 or 1999!

As I sat there staring at the numbers, with the audit partner continuing his endless presentation, I started to feel physically ill. I was sick to my stomach and felt like I might pass out. I immediately got up and headed for the restroom. I am sure the others thought I was headed for a telephone to illegally sell my stock.

After a couple of minutes, I felt well enough to return to the meeting. Thankfully, the accounting presentation was finally over. As the meeting progressed, I was actually treated very well by Haythe, Stanley and the other Board members. I think they actually empathized with the position I was in.

Teri Unsworth, VP of Marketing, was the only other Company employee on the Board besides Stanley. Teri was also the only Board member that I actually liked and respected. She was responsible for all of the national contract relationships with the likes of Marriott, Hilton, etc. My only concern with Unsworth was that she never spoke at the Board meetings unless it was to reiterate her insistence that Guest would lose these large national contracts if we didn't manufacture the amenity products in our own plant. No outsourcing, even if it was cheaper.

Peter Richard was listed in the proxy as an investment consultant. He could have fooled me. I never heard him add anything meaningful to any of the Board discussions. He was somewhat a lightening rod for shareholders due to his frequent sales of his small holdings in Guest Supply's stock.

And then there was Thomas Madison Haythe. It was fairly obvious that Haythe called all of the shots at Guest Supply. No one ever challenged him and of course Walsh and Richard had no incentive to do so. It would have been foolish on their part to do so. They just wanted the Board fees.

Haythe was a bow tie wearing patrician gentleman, approaching sixty years old. He was an Ivy League New Englander all the way and extremely smart. He had his own mid-size law firm on Park Avenue in Manhattan. At one point, I had heard that his middle name, Madison, was a result of his being a descendant of President James Madison. He couldn't have been a direct descendant since President Madison had no children. However, Haythe was married to the daughter of none other than General Charles De Gaulle, former Prime Minister of France.

Haythe, Stanley, Richard, Walsh and Unsworth; it sounded like the passenger list from the Mayflower! I definitely felt like a fish out of water with this group. I doubt any of their relatives were on the steamer to Ellis Island in the 1890's with my ancestors from Minsk!

Towards the end of the meeting, I learned a startling bit of information. The Board had recently engaged Donaldson, Lufkin & Jenrette (DLJ) to sell the Company! I guess one of my suggestions to Stanley at dinner the previous night was already in the works. His resigned mood now made much more sense to me. Rather than continuing to take the constant criticism from shareholders as a result of the Company's constant failure to deliver the expected results, Cliff was throwing in the towel. He was surrendering; not to us but by showing everyone that he really had built a valuable enterprise, despite all of the missteps. After all, he had previously told Sampson that there were numerous "white knights" that would love to own Guest Supply, warts and all.

The decision to engage DLJ was most likely a result of a confluence of several factors that emerged in December of 1997. It was not only my threatened proxy fight but you also had the 13D filing by the Shapiro's. The realization that the problems with Bath & Body Works and the manufacturing plant, and the resulting earnings debacles, weren't going away anytime soon was just icing on the cake.

After the meeting was adjourned, I spoke to Cliff in an attempt to more fully understand the DLJ process and his take on valuation as well as the identity of the potential bidders that were supposedly dying to buy Guest Supply. During our conversation, Cliff tried to get me to empathize with *his* personal situation regarding *his* stock holdings. All the options Cliff was granted in the late 80's had started to hit their expiration dates and Cliff was forced to borrow money from the bank so he could pay the exercise price to the Company, as well as ordinary income tax on the increase in the stock price above the exercise price.

I was amazed that he would somehow try to equate his personal situation with what I was going through with this stock. Of course, now that it was in his personal interest to do so, the Board hired DLJ immediately to try and solve *his* problem. All of the times the shareholders tried to get the Company to take actions, such as a stock buyback, that might help *our* situation, it fell on deaf ears. There was always an excuse; always a reason to say no.

As I was leaving the meeting, I saw the other outside Directors mingling around Paul Xenis, Guest's CFO. I didn't think much of it until I got a phone call from Paul the next day. He said I forgot to get my Board fee check from him after the meeting and he would stick it in the mail. I knew I was entitled to an annual Board fee, but I just assumed it would be one check sent in the mail at the end of each year. Apparently not so with NYSE listed Guest Supply. These other Directors were hovering around Xenis after the meeting to get their handout. Like collecting your fee after selling blood at the local blood bank except these guys didn't even have to give any blood; just a few hours of their time plus they also got a free lunch! I found the practice distasteful and embarrassing. I wonder if Xenis ever did an analysis of the postage saved versus the lost float on the money being paid out sooner.

13

Jilted by Wilmar

As I drove to the Newark airport following the Board meeting, my mind was racing in different directions. At one moment, I was gripped with the fear of a plummeting stock price following the earnings release and the possibility of being wiped out financially due to forced margin sales. The next moment I was elated by the prospect of the Company being sold at a high price. My immediate concern was that Emoff was on my flight back to Columbus and I had to quickly figure out what I would say to him while we waited to board the plane. The earnings wouldn't be released publicly for another ten days and I had to be extremely careful not to disclose any material inside information. The last thing I needed was to get in hot water with the SEC. I had no doubt that Haythe would not hesitate in trying to nail me if he had any opportunity. The only thing that might prevent him from doing so was the little journal I kept on my desk which was becoming filled with incriminating tidbits.

As I walked towards my gate, I was physically and emotionally spent. It had been a long day, to say the least, and I had hardly slept the night before. I tried to stay on an even keel with Todd. I basically told him that, eventually, everything would work out reasonably well with our investment. I couldn't tell him how or when but I did my best to reassure him that it was my feeling that things would work out okay.

Todd didn't press me too much for any details. As a law school graduate, he was well aware of the difficult position I was in. I couldn't help but feel the tremendous pressure I was under. By joining Guest's Board, I had gone from just being one of the many disgruntled major shareholders to a position where I was being looked at as the one responsible for getting all of us out of this nightmare, one way or another. Not only did I have my own financial survival at stake, as well as the responsibility of maximizing the outcome for my clients, I now felt I was also responsible for assuring a positive outcome for Emoff, Sampson, Day and several other large holders, including the Shapiro's.

I had actually left the Board meeting on very good terms with Cliff. I think there was a genuine desire on both our parts to put our past differences behind us and attempt to work together in a positive fashion going forward. In this regard, it was decided that I would be given the opportunity to review the draft of the earnings press release and make suggestions that might help better communicate the Company's situation. My goal was to make sure the release highlighted the many imminent positive developments in the Company's business so that investors would look beyond the disastrous results in the contract manufacturing business.

Our honeymoon was short lived. Without getting into details, our attempt to work together on the press release was a disaster. It didn't help matters that we were both under tremendous pressure as the release date approached. It had been a great quarter for the hotel distribution business but Cliff refused to break out the numbers separately and he refused to have a conference call with shareholders to discuss the release. These were just a couple of items that could have softened the blow to the stock price.

The day before the press release, I was extremely frustrated with Stanley so I decided to call Tom Haythe. He agreed it made sense for us to talk from time to time but when I asked if our discussions could be held in confidence, he said no! In other words, he said I could not count on my private comments to him not getting back to Stanley. I told him I had hoped we could work together for the benefit of all the Company's shareholders, not just for the benefit of Stanley.

I told Haythe that I had very little confidence in Stanley at this point. I wanted Cliff to be held more accountable and to have a timetable for meeting the numerous objectives he outlined for the Board. Furthermore, I felt that Tom and I should be as actively involved as possible in the DLJ sale process due to my lack of confidence in Management.

Not only did my comments fall on deaf ears, Haythe relayed them to Stanley, which further strained our ability to work together, as Stanley felt I was just trying to get rid of him.

The stock price had been hovering in the low teens as the earnings release date approached. The press release went out after the market closed on January 27, 1998. There was very little reaction in the stock price the next day. The huge negative earnings surprise was offset by the generally commonplace knowledge of the DLJ sales process.

Of course, Guest refused to ever publicly announce anything remotely connected to the DLJ initiative. As was the norm for Guest, the Company would never publicly announce anything that they perceived could, in any way, jeopardize their business. The fear, in this case, was that Guest might lose one of their big hotel contracts if it became known that the Company might be sold. Not only did this absurd position hurt the potential sales process by limiting the pool of potential bidders, it also had the potential of keeping investors in the dark. This hurt the stock price which might have reduced the value of a potential bid for the Company. If a bidder thinks a company is worth $20, he may only bid $16 if the stock is trading at $12. If, on the other hand, the stock was trading at $17, he might feel he needs to bid $20 in order to have a chance of being successful. Haythe and Stanley couldn't comprehend this logic.

Despite the lack of a public announcement, the DLJ sales process became common knowledge anyway. Any company is in an impossible situation in a case like this. There are numerous ways that investors become aware without an announcement. For example, the suspension of Guest's stock repurchase plan is a clue that something is happening. It is illegal for a company to repurchase its own shares while it is trying to sell the company. Canceling the earnings release conference call is another clue.

Simply asking management if it has put the company up for sale would force the company to say "no comment." Why say "no comment" if the answer is no? Stanley's comment to Sampson about "white knights" was another hint. The bottom line is that, to the best of my knowledge, none of the Company insiders ever specifically told anyone that DLJ had been hired, yet, by the time the earnings were released, it had become common knowledge.

Six or seven weeks after the January Board meeting, Paul Xenis, Guest's CFO, sent me the confidential information memorandum that DLJ had prepared. This document was given to interested parties after they had signed an agreement not to disclose any of the contents. The document contained non-public information such as sales and earnings projections for the next three years.

I was dumbfounded as I read the projections. The Board had been given the internal projections at the January Board meeting. The projections in the DLJ document were much rosier. For example, the DLJ document had sales rising to $331 million over the next three years even though Xenis's own internal projections presented to the Board had sales rising to only $286 million. Likewise, DLJ had EBITDA (earnings before interest, taxes, depreciation & amortization) hitting $28 million in 2000 while Xenis' numbers projected only $19.9 million.

It appeared that when the goal was to downplay Board expectations so Stanley's performance would look better in comparison, very modest projections were used. When the goal was to get a 3rd party to overpay for the Company, very aggressive projections were used. Welcome to Wall Street. I wondered if an actual buyer of the Company would have had a legitimate cause for legal action if they had seen Xenis's real projections after they had bought the Company based on inflated numbers.

As the months went by, instead of being actively involved in the potential sales process, as I had hoped, I was pretty much kept in the dark. I was given a copy of a preliminary bid by a Philly based apartment supply distribution company by the name of Wilmar. Stanley had mentioned Wilmar to Sampson the prior year as one of the potential 'white knights" that was dying to buy Guest. I wasn't terribly excited by the initial bid of $18 but I felt the number would go higher. Wilmar was intending to pay the purchase price with their stock, not cash. I became concerned that Haythe and Stanley were not thrilled with this non-cash bid and would torpedo the offer. I could understand their desire to not give up control without getting cash but I knew that the major shareholders, including myself, wanted this Company sold at whatever price and terms we could get. We had no desire to wait and see if Stanley could fix the problems. It was too late. It was hard to find anybody that still thought he could do it. He had gotten the Company into an intractable position with the Bath & Body Works contract and there was no way out.

I decided to write a letter to Haythe explaining why I supported the Wilmar offer, if it was the best available. Here is that letter:

Rose Capital
P.O. Box317
Blacklick, OH 43004

Phone 614-939-0166
Fax 614-939-0188

June23, 1998

Mr. Thomas M. Haythe
Haythe & Curley
237 Park Ave.
New York, N.Y. 10017-3142

Dear Tom,

As a follow up to our conversation of June 12th, I thought I should express in writing my thoughts concerning the Wilmar offer. Obviously we all want to "maximize shareholder value." However the definition of this term is not a simple proposition. You have stated that your decision on the offer will be based on whether we will be better off two years from now with or without this merger. We may disagree on the time frame but more importantly we must focus on the risks faced over these two years and the resultant volatility in the share price. Even if I accepted the proposition that not merging with Wilmar could yield a higher share price two years from now, the risks associated with flawlessly achieving management's stated earnings projections of $.60, $.88 and $1.09 for FY 98, 99 and 00 are much greater than the outside shareholders are willing to incur. Furthermore, if these earnings are achieved, I would estimate a $15-$20 share price at the end of the year 2000!

Outlined below are some of the factors I have considered in my analysis:

A. Balance Sheet & Revenue Base

	Guest Supply	Merged Co.
1998 Sales-est.	$237 million	$437 million
Total Assets (3/31/98)	$117 million	$230 million
Net Worth (3/31/98)	*$50* million	$143 million
Net Debt (3/31/98)	$58 million	$24 million

The above chart indicates the merged co. would be much stronger financially than Guest Supply alone. This is relevant for several reasons; The financial strength of the combined companies will allow much more flexibility in growing the business through acquisitions or otherwise. More importantly this strength reduces risk especially if business were to weaken for any reason. Also, the size of the merged co. will attract many new institutional investors that could not have invested otherwise due to their investment parameters.

B. Diversity of Customer Base

Wilmar has a very diverse base of 39,000 active customers vs. Guest Supply's several large national hotel accounts and our very large contract packaging customer.

C. Economy

Guest Supply's business will always be highly subject to the risks associated with an economic downturn. Even the perception that Guest's business is cyclical will cause it to trade at a lower relative valuation. In fact Wilmar's business could strengthen in a recession as housing starts decline and apartments become more in demand due to economic necessity vs. home ownership.

D . Research Coverage/Institutional Ownership

Wilmar has 6 buy recommendations currently vs. none for Guest. If this merger is completed, I believe the size of the combined Company would attract additional institutional ownership plus increased research coverage (possibly Wilmar's advisor Paine Webber). It will be several years before Guest could regain the confidence of Wall St. enough to attract research coverage if ever. This merger will enable us to bury the legacy of missing 10 of the last 11 quarters.

E. Synergy's

While I have not been shown any estimates of the cost saving potential from combined corporate overhead and distribution facilities, I am sure they are significant. Also the potential cross-selling opportunities would be a bonus to an already attractive merger.

F. Price/Earnings Ratio

Management has stated that Wilmar's high P/E ratio would create more risk for us because if earnings targets are missed the P/E ratio will come down. I don't believe Wilmar is trading at an extreme P/E ratio. I would be more concerned if their share price was near 30 as opposed to 23.

There are several reasons why Wilmar will trade at a higher P/E ratio than Guest:

1. Lack of seasonality in their business

2. Much stronger balance sheet

3. Broadly diversified customer base vs. our exposure to several very large customers

4. Consistently meeting earnings expectations vs. our legacy of missing 10 of the last 11 earnings estimates (including the current qtr.)

5. Research coverage and strong institutional ownership

6. Less exposure to a perceived or real economic downturn

7. Earnings volatility due to large customer order patterns for Guest

8. Guest Supply's inability to predict earnings even over very short time frames

As an example of this last item, I would like to recount the fluctuations in the manufacturing budget just since I joined the Board on 1/15/98. At that meeting we were given a gross profit budget for fiscal year 98 showing a loss of $952,000 including the previously reported disastrous Q1. On 4/22/98 we were given a budget for the year showing a loss of $2,192,000 <u>with no change</u> in the sales estimate from the previous estimate. Now it appears that Q3 will be significantly below the 4/22 estimate!

The following grid presents all possible scenarios for a merged company concerning exceeding(E), on-target(T), or missing(M) earnings estimates as if each business were operated separately within the combined Company.

<u>GUEST</u>

W			
I	E/E	E/T	E/M
L			
M	T/E	T/T	T/M
A			
R	M/E	M/T	M/M

I believe that because of all the reasons outlined above that Guest Supply shareholders will be better off in 7 of these 9 scenarios with the exceptions being if Guest exceeds or meets targets while Wilmar misses. I would also like to point out that it is my belief that the likelihood of a significant miss at Guest Supply is much greater due to large customers in hotel and contract.

I have also heard concerns that Home Depot's purchase of Maintenance Warehouse created a competitor which Wlmar will be unable to compete successfully. Obviously this created a formidable competitor but Wilmar's recent results show no signs of this. Last quarter Wilinar reported a same sales person revenue increase of 14% which they expect will increase. Also, the average order size went from $165 to $189 over the past year and from $178 to $189 over the past 3 months while their number of active customers increased from 33,800 to 39,000 over the past 12 months.

In light of all the factors outlined in this letter, it is my opinion that Guest Supply would trade between $8 and $25 over the next 2 years as a stand alone company. I believe as a combined company with Wilmar that the trading range would be $15 to $40. Simply put, I believe that a merger with Wilmar will give us the potential for significant upside while mitigating our downside risk. Therefore, it would be a breach of our fiduciary duty to shareholders not to accept the Wilmar offer. The risk of not doing so is too great and the potential upside of not doing so is limited at best. DLJ, one of the top M & A firms, was unable to generate any bids for the Company despite what appears to be an extensive effort. We must face the reality that due to many factors, many that are outside of our control, the Wilmar offer gives us the best opportunity to maximize shareholder value. We should accept the best Wilmar offer we are able to obtain without further delay. I have seen many companies end up accepting lower offers by delaying hoping that better alternatives would arise. This is a risk we cannot afford to take.

Sincerely,

Barry Igdaloff

As the DLJ process wore on through June and into July, the Yahoo message boards were swirling with takeover rumors. Trading volume in the stock started increasing culminating with the July 21, 1998 Board meeting. The takeover speculators believed that was the day when Guest would announce a sale of the Company.

As the Board meeting convened that morning, the stock traded as high as $19 ¼ on heavy volume, a level not seen since 1996. It was all takeover speculation; certainly the Company's earnings didn't justify that price.

The first item on the agenda was a presentation by DLJ, the Company's investment bankers, to update the Board on the sale process. They stated that the process was over and there were NO bidders! Even Wilmar's preliminary bid had been withdrawn. The Bankers spent a few minutes describing the process and the Companies that had looked at the information. Surprisingly, the two most logical bidders, Guest's main competitor Marrietta and its largest shareholder, the Shapiro's, were NEVER even invited to participate in the bidding!

One of the Board members asked DLJ their advice on what course Guest Supply should pursue at this point. The lead DLJ Banker, who not surprisingly happened to be a close personal friend of Tom Haythe's, responded with a statement I will never forget. He said that since our stock was now up to $19, we should make an acquisition using our overvalued stock as currency. I asked him whether he would give the same advice if the stock was at $10 tomorrow?

The statement just showed how out of touch with reality these Bankers were about the situation. The sickening part was that Guest actually paid significant fees to DLJ for their efforts.

I was too optimistic about the stock price. The takeover fiasco along with June quarter earnings of $.12 vs. $.23 in the prior year cause the stock price to trade as low as $8 1/8 during the remainder of 1998.

On the plane ride home, I drafted a rambling letter to Haythe that summed up my thoughts at the time much better than I could possibly describe them. Here is that letter:

July 22, 1998

Dear Tom,

I wanted to write to express my thoughts concerning the state of affairs at Guest Supply. I am extremely disappointed at the failure of the Board and Management to recognize the risks the Company is incurring and subsequent failure to take the actions necessary to minimize those risks.

I find the circumstances surrounding the Wilmar non-offer very strange. Although I doubt I will ever be able to prove it, I believe that Management never wanted to merge with Wilmar and their inclusion in the process was only meant to encourage a bidding war. Outside of a $25 cash offer, this entire process was only undertaken in an attempt to prove Management's naïve belief that they have created tremendous value for shareholders despite a total of $10 million in profit since the inception of the Company through 9/30/97. Management believed they could "pick up the phone" and get 4 or 5 companies willing to pay $25.

Does anyone really buy into the ludicrous statement that it was good there were no bidders because it means no large distributor wants to enter our business? Since Management has been having discussions with Wilmar for 3 years, this merger would have been completed if Management had really wanted it to happen.

The total failure of the 6 month DLJ process to produce even minimal interest and no bids does not seem to have changed any of the attitudes on the Board. There are Board members who believed the $17 ½ stock price reflected company fundamentals when the DLJ process reflected a $13 or $14 value which generally would represent a premium over the trading value on the stock exchange. What is it going to take for this Board to face the realities of our situation?

Regarding the discussion of my proposal to spin-off the manufacturing division, I will be very surprised if <u>this</u> Board will ever implement this. I regard the discussion at the meeting as lip service and a fulfillment of the legal obligation to hear and discuss ideas presented by a Board member.

Management's view of the Board seems to be to continue to convince them that he has created value. The board seems to buy into this without question. However, the Board seems to be the only ones who do. A majority of the outside shareholders don't, Wilmar doesn't, RCM Capital, Wellington, Pallisades and all the other *former* long term institutional shareholders don't and certainly DLJ was unable to find anyone who does. As for the outside shareholders, it is my opinion that they probably have a higher opinion of the Company's prospects than I do only because they don't have access to the same information as a Board member.

The DLJ process, the spin-off discussion, the shareholder agreement with me and the talk of acquisitions are all just delaying tactics to buy time until Management can stabilize the contract business. I believe we will never consummate an acquisition and I believe, as many shareholders do, it is just a matter of time until the Company has another major disaster, such as losing one or more large contracts in either business or another inventory write-off.

Concerning the effort to obtain new contract manufacturing business, it is my belief that we will get additional business but that this will only offset the loss of existing business. It seems the best we can hope for is 1 ¼ steps forward and 1 step back. What needs to happen for this Board to take the creative steps necessary, such as a spin-off, to minimize the risk to the shareholders?

While the revenue growth in the distribution business is phenomenal, I am skeptical of the potential for it to continue. More importantly, I strongly disagree with Management's constant self-serving comparisons of our margins to paper product distributors. If we are not doing something deserving of these higher margins, then maybe this Company is only worth $13 and we should take an offer at that level.

Due to Management's phobia about full disclosure of margins, shareholders can only evaluate the performance of the Company based on reported earnings and the progress of the share price. Based on these criteria, along with the perceived business risks, Management has failed miserably. Sales and market share gains are only relevant if they produce increasing profits. I would rather do less business if we made more profit!

The answer for me is not just 'if you don't like it, sell my stock," as is suggested to me at every Board meeting. This is not an option for me, just as it is not feasible for you or Management. In fact, it is apparent to me and other shareholders that due to the tax implications and borrowing costs associated with future option expirations, it is actually advantageous to have a low stock price at the exercise date and no sale for at least 12 months thereafter. How is this beneficial to current shareholders?

I realize it is difficult for Management & the Board to make the tough difficult decisions necessary instead of maintaining the status quo, especially when there is either no personal incentive to do so or a disincentive to do so. This is especially true when it requires Management & the Board to admit that mistakes have been made.

In my opinion, any actions that other shareholders might take in light of the failure of this Board and Management to ensure execution of strategies to maximize shareholder value and/or minimize obvious risks would be entirely justified. In that regard, the Company should hire another law firm to handle shareholder matters, as I believe it is an obvious conflict of interest for you to receive legal fees as a consequence of inaction of the Board of which you are a member. It has become obvious to me during our phone conversations that it is difficult to separate your role as corporate counsel from that as a Board member. In fact, you have indicated that your corporate counsel role takes precedence over your Board position.

Sincerely,

Barry Igdaloff

If there was any remaining doubt about my level of frustration with Stanley, Haythe and the rest of the Board, this letter certainly put it to rest.

14

The Phantom Proxy Battle

With the shock of the failed DLJ sale process still fresh in my mind, my thoughts turned to trying to figure out what to do next. One choice was to do nothing and hope that Stanley could fix the contract packaging problems. I was not alone in thinking there was very little chance that Stanley was up to the task. There were no easy answers and he was not the kind of guy to think outside the box and come up with some novel solution to the problem he had created.

Within weeks of the Company's botched or bogus attempt (we will never know for sure which it was) to find a buyer and the subsequent plummeting of the stock price, we bombarded the Company with shareholder proposals for the next annual meeting. We had to come up with new topics as SEC rules prohibit submission of a proposal similar to one submitted the prior year.

Here is a summary of those proposals:

1. A request that the plant be spun-off.

2. A demand that Haythe's golden parachute be rescinded.

3. A demand that Haythe be terminated as general counsel because it is a conflict of interest.

4. Termination of the rights plan or "poison pill"

5. A demand that the golden parachute for Stanley, Xenis, Unsworth & Biber be rescinded.

One of these proposals was submitted by Tom Day. Shortly thereafter, Tom got a phone call from Sampson. Dick informed Tom that Stanley & Haythe had told him that they would use every legal means available against Tom and it would cost him a fortune in legal fees and could possibly cause him to lose his job.

The threat worked. I don't blame Tom. Here he was; a young guy with 2 small children. He had no choice. Of all the things that happened during these 11 years, this threat by Haythe & Stanley was by far the most despicable.

Of course, the Company tried to use every technicality and falsehood known to man in an attempt to exclude these proposals from the proxy materials. The tactics ranged from claiming a deadline was missed even though mailing was done 10 days earlier to 20 page legal briefs submitted to the SEC. Another good month for the Haythe law firm!

Another option left for the shareholders was to get control of the Board in order to bring in new management. Even in light of all the prior missteps, the fall of 1998 represented the most vulnerable time for Stanley and the Board. The DLJ fiasco and the horrendous earnings combined to propel the level of frustration to an all time high.

There were several obstacles to getting control of the Board. First of all, because of Guest's staggered board seat elections, with only two seats up for election each year, it would take two more years to get a majority.

I also knew that Haythe and Stanley would spend as much of the Company's money as necessary to keep control. This would devastate the earnings, causing the stock to drop even further. With many of the larger holders on margin, there was a serious question whether some of us, including me, could survive the fight without being forced to sell our stock.

Dick Sampson implored me not to start a proxy battle. He knew how devastating it would be for everyone involved. He told me point blank that if there was a proxy fight, he would immediately sell all of his stock. I am not sure whether he would have followed through on his threat or not but the mere thought of any of the large shareholders selling their position was enough to scare everyone. The shares were so thinly traded that any large sale would cause the share price to plummet. A huge price drop could start a chain reaction causing more and more margin selling. The end result of such a scenario would be that we would all be forced to sell in the $4 to $8 range and the Shapiro's would end up controlling the Company at a ridiculously low price.

Bob Shapiro had often told me that he felt he was in a win-win situation with his Guest Supply position. If Stanley successfully turned the business around or sold the Company at a high price, he would make a lot of money from his 10% position. On the other hand, if the stock dropped, he could add to his position at prices that he felt were way below the intrinsic value of the business.

The biggest obstacle to waging a successful proxy fight was the SEC group rules. A proxy fight like this one could easily cost several hundred thousand dollars. It may have been possible to raise a war chest from contributions from the ten or so largest shareholders but the SEC proxy rules prohibited this unless we all filed a 13D as a group. There were numerous reasons why this was never going to happen. The bottom line was that one of the major shareholders would have to take on the burden alone. With most of us just struggling to survive the margin calls and client defections caused by the low stock price, the Shapiro's were the only major shareholders that could have pulled this off. While Bob certainly would have encouraged and supported a proxy fight, he never would have been out front of such an effort. He much preferred that somebody else do the dirty work.

When I threatened a proxy fight the year before, I had no idea what was involved. Now I was an expert and the unfortunate reality was that, despite an overwhelming majority of shareholders demanding a change, without a deep pocketed investor to take it on, a proxy fight was a non-starter.

However, I also knew that Haythe and Stanley were extremely paranoid due to the majority of the outstanding shares being controlled by seven or eight extremely angry shareholders. I thought there wouldn't be any risk in a little saber rattling. All that was needed was to get a couple of nominations sent into the Company by the filing deadline; A phantom proxy fight. There was never any intent of actually following through with a full blown proxy contest. The key was never letting **anyone** else know that no one was actually going to follow through with SEC proxy filings, etc. Not even the nominees knew it was never going to go any farther than the one page nomination letter sent to the Company.

Finding two nominees turned out to be more difficult than I had anticipated. The obvious choices like Emoff and Day would never have gotten the approval of their employers, mainly due to their large holdings of Guest Supply stock. Of course, Sampson wanted nothing to do with the whole process. I had to be very careful not to use anybody that was directly connected to me, such as one of my clients, because the shareholder agreement I had signed prohibited me from being involved, unless I gave prior notice to Guest.

I finally found two candidates. One was a broker named Phil Carpenter with Paine Webber in L.A. I didn't actually know Phil but he worked with another broker, by the name of Dan Gallagher, who had a large Guest position for many years. The other was a Rhode Island hedge fund manager named Craig Decesare. Craig's fund held a couple hundred thousand shares of Guest at the time. Besides finding the nominees, I also had to find two other shareholders to actually make the nominations. You can't nominate yourself.

The two nominations were sent to the Company in late October in order to meet the requirements of the Company's by-laws. The next Board meeting was on November 10, 1998. I assumed that since this was the last regularly scheduled Board meeting before January's annual shareholder meeting, that the Board would formally approve the Director nominations to be listed in the proxy. Of course, as part of this process, I also assumed Haythe would inform the Board of the two nominations he had received.

Much to my surprise, the Board nomination process was not on the agenda and the Board was not informed of the two outside nominations the Company had received. If nothing else, I am fairly certain it is a major breach of corporate law to withhold such information from the Board.

After the meeting, I approached Haythe and asked him why the Company's Director nominations weren't approved for the proxy at the meeting. I also told him that I had heard "through the grapevine" that some shareholders had submitted Board nominations. He told me that he had received them and didn't mention it to the Board because he was still reviewing them to make sure they met all of the legal requirements. In other words, my guess is that he wasn't going to broach the whole Director nomination subject until he had figured out what his strategy was for dealing with it.

The shareholder agreement that I had signed a year earlier also required me to vote for the Company's nominees at the 1999 election unless I gave notice within 5 days after the release of Guest's fiscal 1998 earnings (Guest's year-end is September $30^{th)}$ that I did not intend to do so.

The 4th quarter earnings were released on November 25, 1998 and despite a 20% sales increase, earnings declined to \$.28 from \$.33 in the prior year's quarter. Within the 5 day dissent notice deadline, I sent the following letter to the Company:

Rose Capital

November 29, 1998

Mr. Paul Xenis
Guest Supply, Inc.
4301 U.S. Highway One
Monmouth Junction, N.J. 08852-0902

Dear Paul,

I am writing concerning the "Dissent Notice" requirements contained in the Stockholders Agreement dated 12/3/97. As you are aware, this agreement requires me to notify the Company, within 5 days of the release of fiscal 1998 earnings, if I do not intend to vote "in favor of persons nominated as directors by a majority of the current directors of the Corporation for election at the 1999 annual meeting of the Corporation's stockholders."

It is difficult for me to address this issue given that I am not aware of the identity of the Company's nominees. I am surprised the Board did not approve nominees at the last meeting. Given that we are approaching the deadline for giving notice and in order to preserve my ability to exercise my voting rights once I am informed of the nominees, I must inform you that I reserve the right to **not** vote for the Board's nominees. I will make my final decision once the Board has nominated its nominees.

I would like to reiterate that this notice does not mean that I will not vote for the Board's nominees. Also, I am disappointed that the Company has not pursued the provision in the agreement regarding the nomination of a mutually agreeable board candidate. Hopefully we can still resolve these issues for the betterment of Guest Supply. If I can clarify anything in this letter, please let me know.

Sincerely,

Barry Igdaloff

A week later, I received a letter from Stanley stating that the Company did not consider my letter to be a valid "dissent notice" and therefore Guest expected me to honor my commitment to vote for the Company's nominees. The next day, on a Board conference call for the purpose of formally approving the Company's nominees, I abstained from the vote.

On December 11, 1998, Guest Supply filed a lawsuit against me in the Supreme Court of the State of New York for New York County (Manhattan). The lawsuit asked for a preliminary injunction and a temporary restraining order basically seeking to force me to vote all of my shares in favor of the Company's nominees at the upcoming January 21, 1999 annual shareholder meeting.

As I read through the endless pages of the lawsuit, several thoughts went through my mind. First of all, I was enraged by the amount of legal fees Guest was incurring to pursue this ridiculous lawsuit. As a major shareholder, these costs were effectively being borne by me; basically the Company was spending my money to sue me! What made it even more outrageous was the fact that these fees were going to Tom Haythe's law firm.

Haythe was basically advising the Company to incur legal fees, which benefited him personally, and were being incurred to keep him in control of the Company so his gravy train would continue.

However, the most absurd part of all of this was the simple fact that I was being sued to prevent me from voting for Decesare & Carpenter when this was a phantom proxy fight; i.e. a bluff. I was NEVER going to have the opportunity to vote for anyone other than the Company's nominees because nobody was ever going to actually file proxy materials with the SEC!

Of course, the lawsuit only served to further enrage the shareholder base. A message posted on the Yahoo message boards summed it up best; *"Is my understanding of this lawsuit correct? If so, is management really stupid enough to sue one of their largest shareholders or are they actually insane?"*

The hearing before the judge was scheduled for December 22nd. In the meantime, I would get numerous phone calls from the lawyer in Haythe's office that was handling the case. He would constantly try to get me to disclose who my lawyer was so he could deal with him directly. His real intent was to try and find out what my strategy was going to be. Obviously, I had no intention of spending one dime on legal fees for this bogus case but I couldn't let him know that. I refused to give him a name or phone number but told him I would have my attorney contact him directly. He is still waiting for that call.

Since I had no intention of spending the time, effort or money to contest this legal action, I had to make sure Haythe never suspected this fact. My goal was to get the Company to panic and just give us another seat. With the December 22nd hearing date quickly approaching, time was running out. They would have no reason to settle & give us another seat once they got their court injunction forcing me to vote for their nominees. Obviously, the Judge would rule in their favor when I failed to appear at the hearing.

It was obvious that Haythe was worried about possibly not getting the decision he wanted from the Judge. As predicted, on December 14th I received a call from Sampson telling me he had just spoken to Haythe and Stanley. They wanted him to contact me to see if we could come to some type of settlement. I told Dick that I would be willing to listen to what they had to say.

Thirty minutes later, I received the call from Haythe. I immediately told him that I had nothing to do with the Decesare & Carpenter nominations but I would be happy to act as an intermediary between them and the Company in any settlement discussions. I further told him that if he wanted me to do so, I would require a letter from the Company authorizing me, as a Director of Guest Supply, to represent the Company in discussions with Decesare & Carpenter and furthermore such discussions would not be considered as evidence that we are all part of any 13D group.

I had no doubt that Haythe would have loved to have me fall into this 13D trap. Within an hour, I received the indemnification letter from the Company.

My discussions with Haythe were cordial. I began by explaining to him why the shareholders were so upset. The following list is a summary of the grievances shareholders had with the Company:

1. The excessive options grants over the years. The resulting shares made up a larger percentage of the total shares outstanding than any other public company I was aware of. This would have been even worse without shareholder complaints.

2. Lack of insider buying-in fact they were net sellers-even when stock was selling below 20% of sales.

3. Recurring 13D group threats

4. 1997 Thanksgiving Eve change of meeting date.

5. Haythe's golden parachute

6. It seems more Company effort is put into fighting us than proper inventory management.

7. Refusal to meet with large shareholders at their request last August

8. Stock price is ½ of 3 ½ years ago and only because of recent rally.

9. Selective disclosure & material misstatements in private and public disclosures such as SEC filings, conference calls & press releases over many years; too numerous to mention but all documented.

One of the complaints in the lawsuit concerned the requirement in the prior year's shareholder agreement that I use my "best efforts" to get the other large shareholders to also sign the agreement.

I explained that, frankly, the main reason no one else would sign was because of your legal threats; the 13D group threats you had made backfired. It was felt if they signed it could be considered evidence that we all were a group—which we are not. I told him that I used to work for some of these large firms and their corporate legal departments make it difficult to send out Christmas cards, let alone sign a document such as that shareholder agreement. I further explained that I had nothing to hide and that if he was concerned, he should have raised the issue with me last December, not now.

I then indicated to him that our goal was not to get rid of Cliff. We do believe he is capable of operating the hotel business successfully and I know of no suitable replacement nor can any assurance be made that someone better could be found. Also, the disruption caused by any management change is something no one would want to endure. Besides, a minority of the Board wouldn't be able to force a management change even if they wanted to.

After several days of negotiations, a settlement agreement was finally reached. The negotiations lasted all the way up until December 21st, the day before the scheduled court hearing. The last day, negotiations lasted until 2AM! In the final analysis, the whole thing was a non-event.

We were offered a second Board seat to go along with the one that I had. At the last minute, I turned it down. In order to get this second seat, the Company was requiring us to give up all future rights to any additional seats forever! While obtaining a second seat as a result of the phantom proxy fight would, in the short run, have been a huge victory, the long term costs were too great.

I felt that that the ability to ultimately get control of the Board was something we could never give up. We needed this possibility to be constantly hanging over there heads. I think Haythe was somewhat shocked that I turned down his offer of a seat, especially when I did it at the very last minute.

The final agreement was seven pages long. It included a "consulting" agreement for Decesare which paid him $28,000. Coincidentally, he "claimed" to have incurred $28,000 of expenses in preparation for the proxy fight.

As part of the negotiations, I was able to secure a written agreement from the Company that governed my rights should I ever leave the Board. It required the Company to continue to share with me any non-public confidential information if I should leave the Board. Of course, I could not do any trading while I was in possession of any non-public material information. This agreement would prove to be very important in 2000 and early 2001.

15

Dot-Com Mania

As 1999 began, the focus turned to how to improve the valuation of the Company. It was apparent to the shareholders that Guest Supply could not be sold as long as the manufacturing facility continued to generate large losses for the Company. While Cliff Stanley constantly promised new contracts that would correct the problem, we had been hearing that promise for way to long. Spinning off the plant to get it off of Guest's books was actively explored by the Board.

After many months of discussions, the idea was shelved. Various excuses were given but I got the sense that the whole process was just to give Cliff time to fix the problems.

I received a phone call one day, totally out of the blue, from the owner of a fairly large contract packaging facility in California. It seems he had read in Guest's SEC filings that the Company was exploring various ideas to rationalize the manufacturing plant. He said that he had some joint venture proposals that he felt might be beneficial to both parties. I asked him why he was calling me instead of Stanley. He said he had left many messages for Stanley over the last several months and had received no response.

I was livid. The next Board meeting happened to be the following week. I raised the issue to the Board and made a motion requiring Stanley to call this guy from California immediately. Stanley had to be physically restrained from jumping across the boardroom table to get at me. I almost wish the others would have let him do it.

Interestingly, for the first time, Stanley got very little support from his fellow Board members. They were finally tiring of the promises and the heat they were getting from shareholders. When Stanley tried to downplay the significance of the plant by saying we should be focusing on the phenomenal hotel growth, even Tom Haythe had had enough. His retort to Stanley was something to the effect that Stanley had got the Board to dump $30 million into the plant so he had better get it fixed.

I was amazed. After all of the years of blindly supporting Stanley, our constant pounding home of the issue was finally starting to sink in.

As 1999 wore on, the Company's earnings started to improve dramatically. Of course the improvement was coming off of easy comparisons to 1998's disastrous results. But even beyond that, the operating leverage in the hotel business was a big boost as higher sales generated even higher profits as the fixed costs stayed relatively stable.

Also, the numbers from the plant started to improve as additional business was added and efficiency increased. My own projections showed that it was possible that the Company could earn $1, $2 & $3 per share in 1999, 2000 & 2001 respectively.

Normally, these kinds of numbers would eventually lead to a $30 to $50 stock price as investors began to believe in the future earnings potential of the Company. However, something very unusual was happening with the U.S. stock market in the late 90's. We were in the midst of an internet mania. Companies with little or no revenue were trading at billion dollar valuations.

You might wonder what this has to do with Guest Supply. The impact on Guest was twofold. Nobody cared about old economy small-cap companies anymore. The valuations or price earnings ratios on Companies like Guest declined dramatically. On top of this, trading volume, which was never large to begin with, dried up even more. The bottom line is that earnings increases didn't translate into a higher stock price. In fact, after rallying to over $12 at the end of 1998, the stock collapsed again to $8 5/8 during the first quarter of 1999.

To make things even worse, the major market averages were turning in 25% to 30% gains year after year. So here we were stuck in a stock that wasn't moving and had no trading volume so you couldn't sell any size if you wanted to, while the rest of the market was flying.

One of the more egregious examples of the craziness during this time was a Las Vegas based company called PurchasePro. PurchasePro was the poster boy for the mania going on in the business to business or B to B e-commerce arena. The Company went from a market cap of $1.2 billion to bankruptcy in less than 2 years. To add insult to injury, their senior executives went to jail for cooking the books.

This $1.2 billion market cap was achieved on only $65 million of very questionable peak annual sales. The prior experience of the founder and CEO was running a few video stores and health clubs in Ohio.

Despite the craziness of it all, everyone wanted in on the B to B bandwagon and the hospitality supply industry was no exception. All of the big chains such as Marriott, Hyatt, Wyndham and Sheraton announced B to B initiatives.

Towards the end of 1999 and into 2000, I began pushing the Company to get involved in this area. While I certainly didn't believe all of the hype, I did think e-commerce was a natural for Guest's business and I was concerned that the Company's competitive position could get hurt if they were last to the party. At the very least, I thought there might be a way for Guest to get a higher valuation in the market from all of the mania.

Paul Xenis, Guest's CFO, was charged with setting up the Company's e-commerce initiative. On January 18, 2000, after months of diligence, Guest announced a partnership with a Florida based e-commerce portal named GoCo-Op. The site was finally up and running by November, 2000 and GoCo-Op was bankrupt by late summer of 2001. They didn't even make it until 9/11 had a chance to decimate the hotel business.

The window for capitalizing on the e-commerce hype wasn't open very long and no one really thought that Guest's management would be able to take advantage of the opportunity. Routine Company initiatives always dragged on much longer than promised or than they should have.

To try and illustrate the potential for Guest to take advantage of all of the hype, I drafted a hypothetical press release outlining the possibilities. Although it all sounds crazy, press releases such as this weren't that far fetched during 2000. I sent it to Dick Sampson because I knew Cliff Stanley or Paul Xenis would have tried to get me committed to an insane asylum if they had seen it.

Hypothetical Press Release
Guest Supply Completes IPO Of Its E-Commerce Subsidiary

Monmouth Jct., NJ—April 27, 2000—Guest Supply (GSY) announced today the completion of a $120 million IPO of its Business to Business E-Comrnerce unit, Guest B2B (GBTB). Eight million shares were priced at $15 per share representing a 20% interest in GBTB with GSY retaining the remaining 80%. The offering was led by Oppenheimer & Co. with Cruttendon, Roth and Cleary, Gull as co-managers. The offering followed a 20-day 30 city roadshow.

GSY expects to do close to $400 million in revenues this year in its hotel supply business which has grown an average of 25.2% over the last 6 years. The goal of the company is to accelerate this growth rate and ultimately generate 90% of its sales through Guest B2B. Even at historical growth rates the revenue would double in a little over three years. The Company feels that e-commerce will allow its 135 person sales force to be much more productive. Also, e-commerce will allow the company to expand the potential end-market size from the current $2.5 billion to $7 billion by offering maintenance & repair products and furniture through its portal from companies such as W.W. Grainger and Thomasville as well as selling this complete product line to additional end markets such as nursing homes. Additionally, the Company's strong balance sheet will allow it to make strategic acquisitions where appropriate.

CEO Clifford Stanley attributed the success of the offering to investors recognition of several factors that are unique to the Company including GSY's dominant market position in its industry, its established distribution infrastructure including 16 regional distribution centers as well as a long track record of exceptional revenue growth. The offering also allows investors the opportunity to invest in this rapidly growing business without the volatility of GSY's contract manufacturing division.

Analysts note that the $15 offering price appears attractive at 17 times 2003 earnings estimates of 90 cents and 75% of the $800 million sales estimate for 2003. Most other B2B offerings have been priced at much higher valuations. The 90 cent estimate is based on 4.5% after-tax net margins which could prove conservative due to the tremendous cost savings potential of the B2B business model.

The current year earnings estimate for GSY has been revised upward from $1.60 to $3.00 solely as a result of the Company's recently completed tender offer in which 2.5 million shares were repurchased at $20 per share (reducing GSY's outstanding shares to 4.5 million) as well as adjustments to interest costs due to the tender offer and this IPO. The implied value of each GSY share following the IPO is $106 per share based on its 80% stake in GBTB plus $6 of net cash on the balance sheet. GSY closed today at $84 on the NYSE which is 27 times current year estimates and a 25% discount to the implied value. After the close the Company announced a 3 for 1 split of GSY stock.

Based on the most recent proxy statement, the value of CEO Clifford Stanley's 510,338 shares has increased from $7.6 million at year end to $42.9 million based on today's closing price.

Dick found the hypothetical release interesting but even he knew that Guest's current Management would never have the brashness to pull off anything even close to this. Early in 2000, Tom Haythe recognized the potential from the mania when he told Dick the B to B hype could cause the stock to go to $75. Shortly afterward he sold some of his stock in the low teens. Very curious.

16

Bailing Out the Board

In the Spring of 1999, I received a shocking phone call from Dick Sampson. He told me he was quitting his job as a branch manager for Smith Barney. This was not that surprising considering Dick's nomadic relationship with the Brokerage industry. I had lost track of the number of firms and offices he had managed. Every few years he got the itch to move on.

The shocking part was the new job he was taking. Dick was joining Guest Supply as VP of Investor Relations. Of course, in some ways, he had informally been doing this job for Guest for over 10 years. But now he had officially joined the Company.

Dick felt that with earnings finally growing and the Company's problems hopefully behind it, it was time to get the story out. The goal was to raise the market valuation of the Company and then put pressure on Stanley to sell the Company. Even if Stanley had stopped the bleeding in the contract packaging business, the long time shareholders still wanted out. Most of us realized that Guest was way to dependent on Bath & Body Works and there was the fear that the economy would start to slow which would hurt the hotel business.

Dick's huge personal position in the stock certainly justified the move on his part, even if it meant a 70% pay cut. The large shareholders were excited about the move. Somehow, Dick had remained on good terms with Cliff through all the dark years and he was the only shareholder that Cliff listened to and trusted.

From Cliff's standpoint, I am sure he was more than tired of fielding the constant phone calls from unhappy shareholders and was more than happy to let Dick assume the role.

Cliff also had a ton of options expiring later in the year that had been granted 10 years earlier. As Cliff's previous options had expired, he had to borrow from a bank to pay the exercise price plus the ordinary income tax on the difference between the exercise price and the market price. As these loans increased over the years, it became more important for Cliff to keep the stock price high because the loans were collateralized by his stock. If the price fell, he would be forced to sell some. Just like the margin squeezes many of us had experienced when the stock dropped.

With Dick's efforts aided by strong earnings, the stock price rose from single digits up to almost $16 by September of 1999. The stock began to weaken during October, dropping below $14. I wasn't too worried and considered it a normal retracement of the strong up move over the prior 6 months.

A few days before the upcoming November 9, 1999 board meeting, I received a call from Dick. He wanted to meet me for dinner the night before the meeting. I thought it was unusual, given that I would see him the next day and we talked on the phone almost daily. He was driving to Jersey from D.C. so I flew into Philly and he picked me up at the airport. He had made a reservation at Morton's Steak House, again unusual for Dick but this was on the Company's tab.

As we were having drinks before dinner arrived, we made small talk about a variety of issues. I learned from Dick that Tom Haythe's Park Avenue New York law firm was merging with a large, highly respected Toronto firm by the name of Tory's and Haythe was going to be the managing partner of the combined firm. I didn't think much of it at the time, but it would eventually become a key event in the Guest Supply saga.

Then Dick casually brought up what was obviously the reason for our dinner. He informed me that the Company had repurchased 195,000 shares from Stanley, Xenis and Unsworth at $13.19 per share for a total of $2,572,050. 120,000 of these shares were Cliff's. Interestingly, 3 days before the sale, the Company had leaked word of a 100 million tube order from Proctor & Gamble to two of the major shareholders. The leaked information had little effect; the stock price dropped 62 ½ cents in the days immediately prior to the sale, yielding less money to the sellers.

At first I thought he must have been joking, but he wasn't. Apparently, the three officers had a boatload of options that were expiring and they needed to come up with the cash in order to exercise them as well as pay the huge tax bill that was due upon exercise. With the stock dropping, their bank wasn't willing to loan them any more money against their position. A classic margin squeeze. There wasn't enough trading volume for them to sell their shares on the exchange so they had the Company bail them out.

All I could think of was all the times we had begged the Company to do a stock buyback when we were faced with a falling stock price and the resultant margin calls. Now, when they needed help, they had no qualms about having the Company write a $2.5 million check to bail them out. A typical example of what we had felt for years; they ran this Company for *their* benefit, not for the outside shareholders.

We never would have sold into a buyback. We just wanted one so the price would rise, relieving the margin pressure. The only saving grace in this situation was that Management *was* forced to sell their shares at a low price.

Everyone knew that $13.19 was a great buy for the Company and would cause earnings per share to be higher going forward. It made it even sweeter that Stanley had been the one forced to sell. Needless to say, I never wanted to let them know I viewed the move as a positive.

Stanley didn't have the guts to call me directly about the buyback so he had Sampson do it over drinks and steaks at Morton's. Also, the legality of the move was questionable since they called a special executive committee meeting to approve the transaction. You may recall they had set up this executive committee to include five of the seven Directors when I had first joined the Board. Its obvious purpose was to exclude me from any decision making whenever they saw fit. I had gotten them to agree to only use the executive committee if they were unable to get a quorum for the full Board. They apparently decided to ignore that 1998 resolution limiting the use of the executive committee.

The next day at the Board meeting, I could tell they were somewhat embarrassed about the situation. However, that didn't stop me from telling them exactly what I thought of their actions. When I asked for an explanation, Haythe tried to tell me that the personal financial situation of the three Officers wasn't really any of my business. I responded by telling them that spending $2.5 million of the shareholder's money was definitely my business. I asked the Board if the Company will be willing to buy back *my* stock if I ever have a margin call. There was no response.

On the plane ride home, I thought long and hard about what benefit I was getting by being on the Board. If I ever did need to buy or sell any stock, Board members were restricted from trading except during limited windows during the year. I was having very little success in convincing the Board what needed to be done. Since I had secured the disclosure agreement from the Company during the 1998 phantom proxy fight, I didn't need to be on the Board to have access to inside information. As far as participating in Board decisions, it was obvious they would exclude me whenever they saw fit. Also, I felt some comfort knowing that Dick was employed by the Company even though he wasn't actually on the Board.

However, the main advantage to being off of the Board was that I felt I was more of a threat to Haythe and Stanley off the Board than I was on it. Being on the Board legally limited me in many ways. By resigning from the Board, Haythe and Stanley would always wonder why I resigned and what I might be up to. I felt planting this uncertainty in their minds was much more valuable than flying to New Jersey four times a year for those absolutely worthless Board meetings.

The next day I faxed my one sentence resignation letter to Cliff. An hour later I got a call from Dick Sampson trying to find out my reason for resigning. Cliff must have immediately called him to find out what was going on. I told Dick I was disgusted with the insider stock buyback, but he knew there was more to it than that. I played it very coy and kept everyone wondering.

17

Dr. Evil and Mini-Me

The $13.19 stock sale by the Officers of Guest Supply turned out to be the bottom for the stock. As 2000 began, the stock price began a steady climb, helped along by steady earnings gains. Nobody knew who was buying the stock but we weren't complaining.

In early May, Stanley leaked news of a 3 year extension of the Company's Marriott contract which firmed up the stock price even more, causing it to go above $17. No press release was ever issued. Shortly thereafter, SEC filings showed that Stanley had sold another 27,000 shares. I am sure the Marriott leak had nothing to do with his pending stock sale.

With the stock price higher and earnings increasing, thoughts turned to an exit strategy. Even though things were looking up for the Company, the major shareholders were tired; we wanted out. Selling in the open market was never an option. We had too many shares and the trading volume was often non-existent.

We needed some type of takeover. Getting another company to acquire Guest would have been the best option, but after the 1998 DLJ fiasco, we couldn't count on that happening. Another option was an LBO or leveraged buy-out. This involved taking the Company private by raising new equity plus debt to buy out the existing outside shareholders. Current management typically would keep their stock and continue to run the Company.

Rumors about possible LBO's were flying around in the spring of 2000. Of course along with the rumors came the fear that Management would somehow try to steal the Company by paying a less than fair price. In order to try and combat this possibility, one of the major shareholders engaged an LBO firm that he had a prior business relationship with to do an evaluation of Guest's value. They even went so far as contacting Cliff about a potential deal. Their overtures were ignored by Stanley, a risky strategy if he tried to later bring a low-ball offer to the shareholders.

I had approached Bob Shapiro about a possible deal a year earlier when the valuations were much lower. The deal I proposed involved a $75 million preferred investment, $25 million of which would be redeemed over 5 years. The money would be used to buy out 4.2 million of Guest's 7.5 million total shares for $18 per share. At the end of the transaction, Shapiro would have controlled 51% of the stock. Management would have been able to pull $5 million out of the Company while retaining their 20% stake in Guest. Earnings per share would have been much higher going forward due to the reduction in the number of shares outstanding.

As far as I know, the deal never got any serious consideration by the Shapiro's. With the valuations much higher a year later, I saw no reason to try to approach him again.

On April 8, 2000, Dick Sampson informed me that, two months earlier, Guest had hired William Blair & Co. in an effort to sell the Company and that those efforts were ongoing. Of course Dick was aware of the agreement I had with the Company which allowed him to share inside information with me. I was encouraged by the news but I also recalled my unrewarded optimism during the failed DLJ process two years earlier.

Five days later, I received a phone call from an executive at Marietta Corp. by the name of Rick Bloom. He told me that he had heard rumors of Guest Supply's M&A activity and he thought it made sense for the two of us to meet. Things were definitely starting to heat up.

Marietta was based in the middle of nowhere in Cortland, NY. There weren't any reasonable air connections for him to get to Columbus so I agreed to drive up to Cleveland for the meeting. I picked him up at the airport and we drove to a disgusting Denny's located in an industrial section of Cleveland near the airport.

Rick Bloom was a 32 year old investment banker that served as the right hand man for his boss, Barry Florescue, who was 25 years his senior. Both men were somewhat brash and aggressive and they had similar physical builds. It wasn't long before nicknames developed for them in my discussions with Sampson, Day and Emoff; Dr. Evil and Mini-Me.

Dr. Evil was the villain in the Austin Powers spy spoof movies. We used Dr. Evil as a reference to Cliff Stanley's caricature of Florescue, his chief competitor, as a businessman with questionable ethics. Cliff would pass out copies of magazine articles at Board meetings which outlined some of Florescues' alleged former business misdeeds.

Mini-Me was the miniature younger clone of Dr.Evil in the movies so the tongue in cheek nicknames seem to fit perfectly. None of us had any idea whether Florescue was really a shady character. In reality, the fact that Stanley thought he was shady gave us reason to believe that Florescue may have actually been an up and up guy.

It didn't take long during my meeting with Bloom to determine his initial proposal was going nowhere. They wanted to simply merge the two companies, with Guest Supply being the surviving entity. This would have been great for Florescue. He would have eliminated the pricing pressure from his biggest competitor and he would have ended up being the controlling shareholder in the surviving public entity, giving him liquidity that he didn't have as the owner of privately held Marietta.

I told Bloom there were two major problems with his proposal. First, the public shareholders of Guest wanted out. We had no interest in remaining shareholders, with a smaller piece of the pie. We needed a cash transaction that gave us liquidity for our position. Secondly, Stanley would never agree to give control to Florescue in a non-cash deal.

I think Bloom knew his proposal was a long shot but I can't blame him for trying. I suggested that Bloom go directly to Stanley and try to work out an all cash deal. Thus began an 8 month pissing contest between Marietta and Guest.

On June 1st, Marietta sent a loosely worded offer to buy Guest for "up to $24 per share" subject to many contingencies. Guest immediately hired Piper Jaffray to assist in the discussions with Marietta and on June 16th, Guest rejected the "offer" as inadequate.

Basically, the crux of the problem was that Marietta insisted on seeing Guest's confidential business information in order to make a firm offer. They claimed they needed this information in order to see what the cost savings would be from a combined company. The cost savings would dictate how much they could borrow which would dictate the price they could afford to pay. Without the cost data, they said they could only justify paying in the high teens. With it, they might be able to justify paying up to $24 per share.

Of course Stanley had no desire to open up his books to his chief competitor, let alone Barry Florescue. I empathized with Cliff's dilemma but I really didn't think that disclosing the data would have materially hurt Guest's business if a deal never happened.

On June 20th, I received a call from Dick Sampson. Dick told me that he had just accepted a senior executive position with the Founders family of mutual funds in Denver, Colorado. Dick explained it as an offer he couldn't refuse and he also assured me that, one way or another, Guest would be sold.

I was surprised and a little upset that Dick was leaving Guest after barely more than a year. I didn't have a warm and fuzzy feeling about any pending sale of the Company, despite Dick's assurances. It seemed like he was abandoning us in our time of greatest need.

To make matters even worse, in early August of 2000, I received a disturbing phone call from the Charles Schwab & Co. margin department. I had held all of my Guest Supply stock in a margin account at Schwab for the past five years. Despite the stock trading in the $17 to $18 area and the Company reporting record earnings, Schwab had decided that the stock was no longer marginable.

This was a very serious problem for me as I owed over $1 million in margin debt! They said the decision was caused by the steadily declining trading volume in the stock.

The real reason was the internet bubble, which was showing signs of starting to unwind. The big firms had gotten burned on the wild price swings in heavily margined internet stocks with little or no real value. Besides cutting back the marginability of some of these names, they started to panic and began looking for any way they could to reduce their exposure. So Guest Supply popped up in their computer solely based on the low trading volume, despite the fact it was listed on the NY Stock Exchange and actually had substantial earnings and assets.

I only had two choices; sell at least half my position to pay off the margin debt or find another firm willing to extend margin credit to the stock. Selling the stock now, after almost eleven years of agony, was unthinkable and only a last resort; especially with the possibility of an impending buy out. Who knows how far the price may have dropped on a 100,000 share position being unloaded; my guess was to $12 or $13. The lower the price, the more I would have had to sell to pay off the $1 million margin debt.

I spent the next few days on the phone, trying to find another home for my stock. I found several firms willing to extend margin credit to Guest stock but, once they found out the size of my position, they changed their minds.

I had run out of options and was getting hourly calls from the Schwab margin department inquiring about my progress and threatening to sell out the position. Out of desperation, I decided to call Bob Shapiro to see if he could help my situation in any way. I should have done it sooner. Within hours, Bob had arranged for his broker at Bear Stearns to take my position on margin.

I don't know if Bob realized how dire the situation was but I will never forget his willingness to help me when I really needed it.

Once the margin crisis was behind me, I was able to get back to my normal activities of trying to push forward a sale of the Company. The margin crisis made me more determined than ever. Throughout the summer, I would exchange phone calls with Rick Bloom at Marietta. I would call him periodically to see if he was making any progress with Stanley. He would call me whenever he was especially frustrated with being jerked around. His strategy with me, at that point, was to try and get me and the other large shareholders to put pressure on Stanley and Haythe to cooperate with Marietta by giving them access to the information they say they needed.

In mid-August, during one of my phone calls with Bloom, he was ranting about Tom Haythe being a roadblock in the process and how he can't believe Haythe's arrogance, especially after what he did up in Toronto. I was perplexed by the comment and I asked Bloom what he was talking about "in Toronto." He said, "You mean you were on the Board and you don't know about that." I said, "Know about what?" To his credit, he clammed up and wouldn't say anymore.

18

Canadian Escapade

Immediately upon ending the call with Bloom, I did an internet search using the phrase "Haythe and Toronto." Within seconds, fifteen stories popped up on my screen. My jaw dropped as I read the first story below:

Electronic Telegraph (UK)/Wednesday 1 December 1999

Downfall of the 'prissy' lawyer who fondled colleagues

By Philip Delves Broughton in New York and Fred Langan in Toronto

The career of a respected New York lawyer has collapsed after he was accused of fondling and harassing up to a dozen of his female colleagues during a drunken night out.

The profession is astonished that **Thomas Haythe,** 60, a serious, patrician lawyer married to a niece of Charles de Gaulle, can be the same man who appalled Canadian partners with roving hands and lewd jokes. He blames his behaviour on a suspected brain tumour.

Mr Haythe had flown to Toronto with 75 partners from his New York firm to celebrate its merger with a Canadian partnership. A series of "getting to know you" events with the 225 Canadian partners turned sour when Mr Haythe allegedly began misbehaving.

According to Les Viner, managing partner of the newly merged firm, **Tory** Haythe, several women complained about Mr Haythe's behaviour. He told Canada's National Post newspaper: "We have very, very mature women with good judgment. I'm not aware of this being applied on an unwarranted basis." The Post said Mr Haythe behaved "with less decorum than a character in Animal House".

Mr Haythe then apologised the next day but it became clear that he would have to do more as talk of his behaviour swept the legal world. In the course of several meetings he disclosed that he was undergoing tests for a possible brain tumour, which may have caused him to shed more of his inhibitions than he had intended. He was forced to resign and has returned to his home outside New York.

The incident has garnered widespread attention in Canada, particularly exciting those hostile to the tide of American firms flooding the country. For them, Mr Haythe has become an unfortunate symbol of the evils of American commercial colonialism in Canada.

Last week, Mr Haythe made the embarrassing visit to his father and step-mother in Greenwich, Connecticut, to explain. Frances Haythe said: "He just said he apparently had too much to drink but he doesn't remember. He's not a heavy drinker. I've never seen him drink more than two glasses of wine.

"I have great difficulty believing he became blotto. It sounds to me like somebody spiked his drink. I can't believe it. He's so proper, really prissy proper."

Mr Haythe's wife, Sabine, is standing by her husband and is angry at the treatment he has received. She said: "I'm so angry about what people are saying about him. We can't explain it. He can't explain it. Things in life are bizarre sometimes.

"It's a very sad story and [the resignation] should never have happened the way it happened." She said the allegations have been devastating to the couple. She said: "It's a horrible story. It's a nightmare. I don't even think something like this could have happened. It's more than we can handle."

As I stared at my computer screen, I thought I must be dreaming or hallucinating. Not that incidents like this don't happen on a fairly regular basis in the corporate world, but this was Tom Haythe. The 60 year old, bow-tie wearing, Harvard educated Connecticut aristocrat. The Thomas Madison Haythe that I knew was the last person on earth that I would have thought would be capable of this. Haythe was always so in control.

Interestingly, Haythe received no support from his long time partners as evidenced by the following excerpt from one of the articles I found:

'There was no dissent among the U.S. members of the firm when it came to taking action against Mr. Haythe. There was none. Absolutely none. Everybody agreed, unanimously, quickly and decisively, that it was intolerable."

Another sad example of how one brief slip up can erase decades of hard work and permanently ruin a reputation.

One of my initial thoughts turned to how it was possible that I was just learning of this November 1999 incident, nine months after the fact. I was in contact, on a daily basis, with a dozen or more money managers all over the country. And each of them was in contact with dozens of their own clients regularly. How was it possible that *none of us* had gotten wind of Haythe's escapade? This is a question I could never answer other than to say that while the story was all over the Canadian papers, it somehow wasn't publicized in the U.S.

After I regained my composure and assured myself that I wasn't dreaming, I immediately called Sampson as I faxed him several of the news stories. He was as flabbergasted as I was. After all, Dick prided himself on being in the loop as far as every bit of information surrounding Guest Supply. He said he would call me back after he got a hold of Cliff.

Dick called me back about fifteen minutes later. He said his call with Stanley was one of the strangest he had ever had. Cliff put him on hold for a few seconds then proceeded to tell Dick that Tom Haythe has been extremely important to Guest Supply for nearly twenty years and that he is still the Company's general counsel. Cliff told Dick that Haythe thinks someone must have spiked his drink! No more mention of a brain tumor!

Dick said Stanley's comments sounded like he was reading from a prepared statement. Dick suspects he was put on hold while Stanley located the document buried somewhere on his desk. He probably thought after nine months he never would have to use it.

After digesting the situation for a few hours, I started to grasp that this incident had the potential to be of much more significance to the Guest Supply shareholders than it first appeared. While the investment banking process and the Marietta overtures seemed to indicate that Guest might be sold, long time shareholders like me were very skeptical that it would ever happen. We had been conditioned over the years to look at Guest as being controlled by an entrenched Board and Management that really had no interest in doing anything other than making sure they remained entrenched for their own benefit. Many of us felt that the DLJ process in 1998 and the current "exploration of strategic alternatives" was just for show. We felt they would never do anything unless they were forced to.

I felt this Haythe 'incident" changed the whole equation. Miraculously, once he found out that I knew about Toronto, he started to promptly return my phone calls and actually shared substantive information with me about the potential sale process. I honestly believe, as a result of the Toronto incident, that Haythe felt if Guest remained a public company with hostile shareholders, this Toronto incident would constantly be hanging over his head. I think he now wanted it to be over, just like we did, albeit for different reasons.

Taking nothing for granted and desiring to keep as much pressure on the Company as possible, I sent the following letter to Cliff Stanley on August 16, 2000:

Rose Capital

August 16, 2000

Mr. Clifford Stanley
Guest Supply
PO Box 902
4301 U.S. Highway One
Monmouth Junction, N.J. 08852-0902

Dear Cliff,

I have recently become aware of the situation regarding Tom Haythe outlined in the enclosed article. As a former Board member and long time major shareholder, this incident and the Company's response(or lack thereof) concern me greatly. First of all, I am astonished that the proxy material made no adequate disclosure of Tom's resignation from the 300 person law firm that bears his name and which provides legal counsel to the Company, especially given that Tom was standing for election to the Board. Also, the proxy makes no mention of Tom's current employment or occupation.

You are well aware that many shareholders have been concerned about the inherent conflict of interest from Tom's dual role as Board member and General Counsel. There is nearly universal outrage at the $270,000 golden parachute negotiated by the Company without the aid of independent counsel. I have never seen such an arrangement in my over twenty years of analyzing and investing in small-cap public companies.

I certainly have no desire to cause Tom any further embarrassment or humiliation but I suggest that the following steps be taken immediately:

1) Tom should resign his Board seat.

2) Tom's general counsel employment agreement (including the $270,000 golden parachute provision) should be terminated under the moral turpitude clause included therein.

3) The Company should repurchase all shares and options from him (using the last twenty days average price or something similar).

I know you believe that Tom has been very important to the Company for the last 18 years but we need to consider the potential business risks going forward if theses actions aren't taken. Are the employees of Guest aware of this situation? What if Marriott, BBW or other customers hear about this'? What effect could this have on our business? A shareholder asked me the question; What action would have been taken if we were General Motors instead of Guest Supply? Other shareholders have suggested that we have a special shareholders meeting to discuss this matter. I hope this isn't necessary, but if it is, I believe there would be overwhelming support for the steps outlined above. I look forward to hearing your thoughts.

Sincerely,

Barry lgdaloff

I didn't really expect a response from Cliff but I felt it was important to leave this matter hanging over their heads as they went through the potential sales process. To reinforce the Company's obligation to keep me up to date on the process, as well as state my views on their failure to cooperate with Marietta, I sent the following letter to Tom Haythe in early September:

Rose Capital

September 7, 2000

Mr. Thomas Haythe

Dear Tom,

I appreciate your taking time last week to discuss some of my concerns regarding Guest Supply. I wanted to reiterate my views on some of the issues we talked about. Regarding my non-disclosure agreement with the Company executed 12/22/98, I want you to know that I take very seriously the representations I made as to non-disclosure or use of any material information I receive from the Company. Likewise, I expect the Company to fully cooperate with my desire to "remain apprised of the strategic and other material developments involving the Company."

Regarding the discussions with our largest competitor, I am certainly aware that the Company shouldn't be cavalier in disclosing non-essential information. However this concern should not be used to prevent a transaction from occurring. Your contention that Guest's public filings contain sufficient information to determine the cost savings available in a merger is ludicrous. I am sure you don't really believe it. If you do, I would like a call from Guest's Investment Banker to explain this to me directly. Because of the micro-cap size of the two companies, detailed due diligence is essential, not unlike our purchase of NASCO. I am afraid the real problem is Management simply is not willing to sell to this buyer despite your stating otherwise. You alluded to some interest from another public company. I suspect this is another attempt to delay negotiating in good faith with the only company that has expressed a real interest.

Tom, the liquidity(trading volume) in GSY is not at a level which warrants this Company remaining public and it is steadily declining. I would be happy to outline the factors which are causing this problem. I can assure you that changing Specialists or leaving the NYSE are not solutions. Despite the growth the Company has had, a $135 million market cap doesn't even get us close to being considered a small-cap vs. a micro-cap due to the fact that the market cap required to be considered a small-cap keeps going up faster than our increase. Therefore we are falling further and further behind. Guest is too small and too illiquid to warrant any material institutional interest or research coverage. It is not inconceivable that if Guest earns $1.80 next year that the stock could trade at 8 to 9 times or $14.50 to $16.25 at THE END OF NEXT YEAR. If the market corrects or there is even talk of a recession or if we miss earnings targets, etc., the stock will be even lower. I believe these risks far outweigh the concern that our largest competitor might obtain information which MIGHT have any material effect on our earnings. Furthermore, this competitive risk disappears if the Company successfully consummates a merger, which I believe would happen if not for the Company's reluctance. In summary, the risks to the shareholders of not selling the Company are huge compared to any possible benefit of not doing so.

I hope to hear from you soon regarding how the Company intends to address and/or resolve these issues and concerns.

Sincerely,

Barry Igdaloff

A week later I received the following cordial response from Haythe on his new stationary:

LAW OFFICES

OF

THOMAS M. HAYTHE
5TH FLOOR

90 PARK AVENUE

New YORK, NEW YORK 10016

TEL (212) 210-9583

FAX (212) 210-9444

September 13, 2000

Mr. Barry Igdaloff
Rose Capital
P.O. Box 317
Blacklick, OH 43004

Dear Barry:

Thanks for your letter of September 7, 2000. I always appreciate hearing your views.

We are pleased you take very seriously your representations to the Company in the December 22, 1998 letter. The Company will, to the extent consistent with its contractual and other legal obligations, cooperate with you as contemplated in that letter.

Please feel free to contact me at any time.

Best regards.

Sincerely,

Thomas M. Haythe

19

The Bottom of the Ninth

Throughout the fall of 2000, rumors were swirling among the shareholders as to what was really going on. Helping to increase the frenzy were comments Cliff had made on two separate October 24th phone calls he had with a couple of large holders. They both relayed the same quote to me; Cliff told them he would buy the stock now, if he could. If that statement wasn't an indication that the Company was in the end stages of favorable buyout talks, nothing was.

On November 16th, Marietta decided they were getting nowhere and decided to turn up the heat. They sent the following letter to Stanley, which now claimed they were willing to pay $21 and were also submitting two nominees for the two Board seats that were up for reelection at the January 2001 annual meeting:

PROPOSAL MADE TO ACQUIRE SHARES OF GUEST SUPPLY, INC.

By letter dated November 16, 2000, BFMA Holding Corporation made a proposal to Guest Supply to acquire all of the shares of Guest Supply not currently owned by BFMA at a price of $21.00 per share in cash. The text of the proposal letter is set forth below:

  BFMA HOLDING CORPORATION
  50 EAST SAMPLE ROAD, SUITE 400
  POMPANO BEACH, FL 33064

November 16, 2000

VIA FACSIMILE AND FEDERAL EXPRESS

Mr. Clifford W. Stanley
Chairman and Chief Executive Officer
Guest Supply, Inc.
4301 U.S. Highway One
Monmouth Junction, NJ 08852-0902

Dear Mr. Stanley:

BFMA Holding Corporation is currently the beneficial owner of 308,600 shares of Guest Supply, Inc.'s common stock (representing 4.7% of the issued and outstanding shares, based on Guest Supply's most recent public filings). BFMA is prepared to offer $21.00 per share in cash for each share of Guest Supply it does not already own. This proposal represents a premium of approximately 25% over the closing price of Guest Supply's common stock on November 16, 2000 and a premium of approximately 29% over the average closing price of Guest Supply's common stock over the last 20 trading days ending on November 16, 2000.

Since 1997, BFMA has consistently expressed its interest in combining its operating subsidiary, Marietta Corporation, with Guest Supply. On a number of occasions you communicated to representatives of BFMA that Guest Supply was available for sale. However, each time we have approached you with a serious expression of our interest, you dismissed our proposals as inadequate.

In early May 2000, representatives of BFMA discussed with you BFMA's desire to acquire Guest Supply. You inquired at that time as to the price per share that BFMA would be willing to pay and suggested that BFMA formally request certain information to assist in that determination. We preliminarily indicated to you our thoughts on the value of the company and in mid-May formally requested information to assist in confirming such value. None of the requested information was provided. On June 1, 2000, I wrote a letter to you and your directors on behalf of BFMA, formally proposing to acquire the shares of Guest Supply for $24.00 per share in cash. The closing stock price of Guest Supply's common stock on May 31, 2000 was $17.56 per share. On June 16, 2000, we received a letter from you indicating that you rejected our proposal as "inadequate." Although discussions continued and correspondence was exchanged over the next four months, very little progress was made. As you are well aware, we communicated to you and your representatives on numerous occasions our growing frustration with respect to the lack of such progress. On September 20, 2000, you sent us a letter terminating discussions with BFMA and confirming our belief that you never seriously intended to cooperate with us in exploring a transaction.

As a result of your dismissal of our prior proposal, we have officially nominated two directors for election as Class C Directors of Guest Supply at Guest Supply's 2001 Annual Meeting anticipated to be held on January 17, 2001.

The nominees for director are Logan D. Delany, Jr., an independent investor and businessman, and Charles W. Miersch, the Senior Associate Dean of the Simon School of Business at the University of Rochester. Messrs. Delany and Miersch have consented to serve as directors and, if and when elected, have announced their intention to form a special committee of directors and hire independent financial and legal advisors to explore a prompt sale of Guest Supply to the highest bidder.

Since our discussions earlier this year, the markets have been volatile and valuations have deteriorated. Despite this deterioration, we remain interested in pursuing a transaction with Guest Supply. We believe that the combination of Marietta Corporation and Guest Supply is a strategic fit and will allow the combined company to benefit from our complementary capabilities. From publicly available information, we have identified a number of areas in which cost savings can be implemented and operating efficiencies can be achieved. We hope to be able to confirm such savings through due diligence. Moreover, we would anticipate that the transaction would substantially increase the business of the combined company at each of the current operating locations.

Finally, we believe that a transaction can be completed quickly, without regulatory issues, and we will devote all necessary resources to accomplish this goal. We are prepared to quickly negotiate a definitive agreement with respect to our proposal.

We were hoping to negotiate a transaction on a cooperative basis; however, we are now prepared, if necessary, to remove you from the decision process and appeal directly to the Guest Supply shareholders.

If you would like to discuss this proposal further, please do not hesitate to call me or Rick Bloom.

Sincerely,

BFMA HOLDING CORPORATION

Barry W. Florescue
Chairman of the Board and President

This letter was a declaration of war by Florescue and Stanley took it as such, although he still wouldn't budge in opening up his books to Marietta. Cliff naively believed that there was no way the Marietta nominees would win the two board seats, if it got that far. My view was that there was no way that Stanley would win that vote. Even if electing the Marietta nominees wasn't in the best interests of the shareholders, most still would have voted for them, just out of their frustration with Stanley. Ironically, Cliff himself was one of the two Guest nominees up for reelection.

Our goal was to get Sampson to convince Stanley that he had no chance of winning the election and therefore he better strike a deal with someone, before it was too late. Having two Marietta representatives on his Board was way more than he could have tolerated. Sampson tried to hammer home the reality to Stanley but Cliff never would admit to Dick that he might lose the vote. No one was sure what he really thought. If he did think he might lose, I am sure he would never let anyone know.

On December 18, 2000, Stanley sent the following letter to the shareholders, personally attacking Florescue and enclosing the same negative 1987 Forbes article he had previously passed out to the Board:

December 18, 2000
Dear Fellow Shareholder:

> As you may know, BFMA Holding Corporation, the parent company of one of Guest Supply's principal competitors, has filed a Proxy Statement with the Securities and Exchange Commission in order to solicit proxies to elect two BFMA nominees as Class C directors at our next Annual Meeting of Shareholders. BFMA's Proxy Statement also says that it has "proposed" to pay $21 per share for all the outstanding shares of Guest Supply common stock that it does not already own.
>
> BFMA's Proxy Statement is not an offer for your Guest Supply stock, nor has BFMA demonstrated that it has the financial ability to make an offer. If BFMA wants to purchase Guest Supply stock, and if it has the financing to do so, it is free to make an unequivocal offer based on the comprehensive information about the Company that is publicly available and BFMA's own in-depth knowledge of our industry.
>
> We plan to mail a Proxy Statement containing reasons why you should not vote for BFMA's nominees. In the meantime, we believe you should consider the following information:
>
> BFMA has never made a formal offer to acquire Guest Supply and has not demonstrated an ability to finance a purchase at $21 per share.
>
> BFMA is the corporate parent of our principal competitor in the lodging amenities business, Marietta Corporation, and is controlled by Barry W. Florescue.
>
> We believe that Mr. Florescue has a track record of acting contrary to shareholder interests and for his own financial gain, which leads us to question his true motivation.
>
> BFMA's nominees for the Guest Supply Board of Directors, Logan D. Delany, Jr. and Charles W. Miersch, are directors of BFMA and of Marietta, and Mr. Delany's company, Delany Capital Management Corp., is an investor in Marietta. We are convinced they would not represent the interests of all Guest Supply shareholders.
>
> Guest Supply has delivered on its strategic plan and is financially strong.
>
> In June 2000, Guest Supply retained financial advisers, U.S. Bancorp Piper Jaffray, to assist the Company in exploring strategic alternatives.

Your Board believes that, based on its discussions with BFMA dating back over two years, and its knowledge of Mr. Florescue's track record, BFMA is attempting to entice you to vote for its director nominees with an illusory proposal to purchase stock that may never be realized. Your Board also believes that BFMA's nominees, if elected, may pursue a strategy in the interests of BFMA, Marietta and Florescue, rather than in the interests of all Guest Supply shareholders.

BFMA Has Not Made an Offer to Acquire Guest Supply and Has Not Demonstrated an Ability to Finance a Purchase at $21 Per Share

In its proposal, BFMA says it is "prepared" to pay $21 per share for Guest Supply common stock, but we doubt it will ever actually do so. It says it expects to achieve "cost savings" by combining Guest Supply with Marietta and that it hopes to be able to confirm such savings through due diligence. If—as we expect—the necessary cost savings cannot be confirmed through due diligence, BFMA will presumably re-evaluate its position and either reduce the sum it says it is "prepared" to pay (as it has already done once, from a possible $24 per share to a possible $21 per share) or decline to make any offer.

From June until September of this year, we had extensive discussions with BFMA, based on BFMA's then-stated intention to offer $24 per share for the Company's stock. In June, we retained U.S. Bancorp Piper Jaffray to assist us in our negotiations with BFMA and to explore other strategic alternatives. We pursued our discussions with BFMA seriously but, after over three months of effort, we terminated negotiations for several reasons, including: (i) our concerns over BFMA's repeated requests for competitively-sensitive information while refusing to sign a Confidentiality Agreement, which it said on several occasions it would sign; (ii) the unresolved issue of how the transaction could be financed, particularly in light of BFMA's stated need to identify at least $10 million in synergies or cost savings to finance the deal; and (iii) a growing distrust of the true motivations of BFMA and Mr. Florescue.

Now, BFMA has come back with a possible offer to purchase Guest Supply at a lower price in the context of a proxy fight, stating that it may seek to recoup the cost of a proxy contest (which it estimates will be approximately $500,000) from Guest Supply.

BFMA's Nominees Would Be Paralyzed by Conflicts of Interest

BFMA's nominees, Messrs. Delany and Miersch, are directors of BFMA and Marietta. In addition, Mr. Delany's investment company, Delany Capital Management Corp., lists Marietta as one of its "portfolio companies"—a fact that BFMA and Mr. Delaney have not disclosed in their proxy statement.

As nominees of our principal competitor, Messrs. Delany and Miersch would be hopelessly conflicted in most important decisions of the Company, including all matters that would affect our competitive position in the lodging amenities market.

Moreover, as nominees of a shareholder with an expressed intent to acquire theCompany, they would have conflicts regarding their purported objective of arranging for a sale of the Company. Our shareholders should seriously consider whether BFMA's nominees would be motivated to assure the highest price for Guest Supply's shareholders, or—as we fear—the lowest price for BFMA.

Indeed, the conflict between BFMA's interests and our shareholders' interests is already apparent. We are concerned to hear that Marietta is already attempting to subvert our relationship with at least one long-term customer by telling them not to sign a contract with Guest Supply because

Marietta will eventually own us.

Florescue is Not Likely to Enhance Shareholder Value

According to an article published in Forbes in June 1987, after Mr. Florescue took control of Horn & Hardart through a proxy fight, he drew an annual cash salary of $850,000 but did little to enhance shareholder value. The Forbes article goes on to say that a company co-owned by Mr. Florescue received $1.2 million from Horn & Hardart over three years for the use of two corporate jets.

According to the Forbes, article "Why Didn't They Pay Him To Stay Home":

"Last year [1986] … Horn & Hardart Co. lost $28.4 million on $405 million in revenues.… How did the company go so far astray? Look no further than Barry Florescue, 44, who has been Horn & Hardart's chairman and chief executive officer since 1977."

"However poorly the company does, Florescue seems to be doing just fine."

A copy of the Forbes article is enclosed.[1]

---

1.   Forbes, on behalf of itself and the author, has consented to the use of a reprint of the article as proxy soliciting material. The participants have paid Forbes for the rights to reprint the article.

In 1996, the United States Office of Thrift Supervision ("OTS") filed civil charges against Mr. Florescue, according to a press release by the OTS. The OTS alleged that when he controlled Century Bank, a Florida Savings and Loan Association, Mr. Florescue illegally used bank assets for his personal use. On June 14, 1996, the Sarasota Herald-Tribune reported that Mr. Florescue allegedly had Century Bank buy a Lexus automobile for his use which he then transferred to his wife; took compensation before it was earned, received reimbursement from the bank for travel and personal expenses not for the benefit of the bank, and caused the bank to lend him money on favorable terms. Mr. Florescue's lawyer was quoted in the June 15, 1996 edition of the Sarasota Herald-Tribune responding to the charges by explaining that, prior to the OTS filing of formal charges, Mr. Florescue had paid the bank back for the vast majority of the questioned items.

Lastly, Mr. Florescue's company, BFMA, has a history of decreasing its offer as a potential transaction progresses. In 1995, BFMA acquired the stock of Marietta at $10.25 per share after having previously made a bid of $12.30 per share, according to The Reuters Business Report on August 28, 1995. BFMA "proposed" $24 per share for Guest Supply this summer and its latest proposal is for a "possible" $21 per share. You should be concerned that if BFMA ever does make a real offer, once all contingencies are removed, the amount offered might be substantially less than even the latest proposal.

Guest Supply is Financially and Strategically Strong

The Board of Directors and management of Guest Supply continue to act to build value for ALL shareholders. Fiscal 2000 proved that the Company is financially and strategically strong:

Sales growth of 20.7%

Net income increased 35.5% to $1.44 per diluted share

Operating margins increased from 5.1% to 5.6%

Operating income increased 32.9%

In August 2000, the Company entered the market for furniture, fixtures, and equipment with the creation of Guest Purchasing Services. Adding the FF&E products expands our potential market from approximately $2.5 billion to over $7 billion

Announced the launch of the Company's business-to-business e-commerce site, www.guestsupply.com

Engaged U.S. Bancorp Piper Jaffray to pursue and recommend other strategic alternatives

Your Board of Directors urges you not to take any action concerning BFMA's nominees until you have had a chance to review Guest Supply's proxy materials. We also urge you to read and compare these materials carefully and then decide who is truly acting independently in your best interests.

In order to provide sufficient time for shareholders to consider the merits and risks of BFMA's proxy solicitation, your Board of Directors intends to reschedule the Annual Meeting. When the Annual Meeting date is set, shareholders will receive a Proxy Statement from Guest Supply, containing detailed reasons why you should not vote in favor of BFMA's nominees.

Sincerely,

/s/Clifford W. Stanley

Chairman, President & Chief
Executive Officer

It was apparent that Haythe and Stanley were pulling out all the stops in their effort to discredit Florescue and win the vote. Of course, Florescue couldn't let Stanley's attack on him go unanswered. Here is his January 8, 2001 response which was the final salvo in their battle:

January 8, 2001

Dear Fellow Shareholder:

PROTECT THE VALUE
OF YOUR INVESTMENT IN GUEST SUPPLY, INC.
Several weeks ago, we sent you a proxy statement and BLUE proxy card in connection with the upcoming meeting of Guest Supply shareholders. BFMA has been a holder of a substantial number of shares of Guest Supply for some time and currently seeks your support in order to effect important changes at Guest Supply. We believe that the management of Guest Supply and its Board of Directors have not been acting in your best interests. It is time now to make sure the Board is focused on maximizing shareholder value for ALL Guest Supply shareholders. To protect your investment, we urge you to sign, date and return the enclosed BLUE proxy card TODAY.
You may also have recently received a mailing from Clifford Stanley, the current Chairman and Chief Executive Officer of Guest Supply. We believe that

his letter was a blatantly misleading attempt to distract your attention from the real issues in this election. In our letter to you today, we want to set the record straight.

YOUR VOTE FOR THE BFMA NOMINEES
IS A VOTE FOR THE SALE PROCESS

BFMA has made an offer to acquire Guest Supply for $21.00 per share; however, we are not asking you to vote on our offer. We are requesting that a sale process be initiated and that BFMA be given a fair chance to participate in that process. If another bidder emerges to purchase Guest Supply at a higher price, BFMA will either increase its offer price or bow out of the bidding contest. If BFMA is ultimately the highest bidder in the process, you can decide at a later date whether to accept the proposed transaction OR retain your current investment. This proxy fight is about the sale process—not about price.

You have a simple but important choice to make: you can support the status quo and suffer with a low multiple, low value and illiquid stock OR you can elect the BFMA nominees, telling Guest Supply's management and Board that you are tired of their delay and you want the company to truly explore a sale— NOW.

The BFMA nominees are committed to affording the Guest Supply shareholders, the TRUE owners of the company, the opportunity to consider BFMA's offer as well as any other potential transactions that would provide a greater value to Guest Supply shareholders. BFMA has offered to purchase all of the shares of Guest Supply for $21.00 per share in cash; however, BFMA has continued to state that we would consider offering a higher price if Guest Supply's management and Board were able to demonstrate value not apparent in the publicly available information.

We believe that, if you vote for Mr. Stanley and Teri Unsworth, the incumbent Board will continue to resist exploring real opportunities to maximize the value of your shares. This is especially true if the opportunities do not also serve their self-interest. We are convinced that the incumbent Board and management are not acting in your best interest.

WHAT IS GUEST SUPPLY HIDING?

On November 16, 2000, BFMA sent a letter to Mr. Stanley and the Board offering to acquire all of the shares of Guest Supply, at $21.00 per share in cash. At the same time, BFMA nominated Logan D. Delany, Jr. and Charles W. Miersch to run against Mr. Stanley and Ms. Unsworth at Guest Supply's 2001 Annual Meeting to be directors of Guest Supply. At the time, Guest Supply's 2001 Annual Meeting was scheduled for January 17, 2001, according to the New York Stock Exchange. In late November, Guest Supply postponed the meeting to February 9, 2001 and has now recently informed the New York Stock Exchange that the meeting has been postponed indefinitely, to a date "to be determined." Not only has Guest Supply indefinitely postponed the meeting, it has not even filed any proxy materials with the SEC.

What are they hiding from you? What don't they want you to know? Why are they delaying the vote on the election of directors? Is this Board really interested in maximizing shareholder value or only in their own self-interest? The only public communication from Guest Supply you have received is Mr. Stanley's letter to shareholders dated December 18, 2000, in which he makes claims which we believe are untrue and misleading.

GUEST SUPPLY'S STOCK PERFORMS VERY POORLY

MR. STANLEY CLAIMS: "The Board of Directors and management of Guest Supply continue to act to build value for all shareholders."

THE TRUTH IS: Most shareholders have not done well at all. This proxy contest is as much about Guest Supply's poor share price performance during Clifford Stanley's nearly fifteen years as a senior officer of Guest Supply as it is about BFMA's commitment to maximize shareholder value through a fair and efficient sale process. The share price today is LESS than the share price of Guest Supply's common stock when Mr. Stanley took over as Executive Vice President and Chief Financial Officer in April 1986.

Guest Supply's feeble return to shareholders over the last few years is indisputable. The graph below demonstrates that, although the share price may have risen recently, the performance of Guest Supply common stock over the last five years, relative to alternative investment opportunities, has been terrible.

A $100 investment in Guest Supply's common stock on December 31, 1995 was worth approximately $74.59 on December 31, 2000, a 25.4% loss—a 25% loss during one of our nation's greatest periods of growth and profitability. If you had invested the same $100 in the S&P 500 Index, the Russell 2000 Index or the Dow Jones Industrial Index, your investment would have been worth $214.36, $153.03 and $210.80, respectively. This means that your investment would have been worth 2–3 times your investment in Guest Supply. The following chart, which compares the price performance of the common stock of Guest Supply, the S&P 500 Index, the Russell 2000 Index and the Dow Jones Industrial Index, illustrates the point. The comparative price performance has been calculated as of December 31 of each year for the last five years and assumes an initial investment of $100 on December 31, 1995.

FIVE-YEAR COMPARABLE PRICE RETURNS

	1995	1996	1997	1998	1999	2000
Guest Supply	$ 100	$ 78	$ 58	$ 53	$ 66	$ 75
S&P 500	$ 100	$ 120	$ 158	$ 200	$ 239	$ 214
Russell 2000	$ 100	$ 115	$ 138	$ 134	$ 160	$ 153
Dow Jones	$ 100	$ 126	$ 155	$ 179	$ 225	$ 211

Is this what Mr. Stanley believes is "building value for all shareholders?" While BFMA has invested over $5,000,000 in cash to purchase Guest Supply common stock, Mr. Stanley and the other executive officers and directors received most of their currently held shares through the exercise of options and warrants. Many of these options and warrants were "net exercised" which means that management and the Board did not have to pay any actual cash for their shares of stock. Therefore, even though Guest Supply share price performance has significantly lagged behind the overall markets, the executive officers and directors have made money through their options and warrants, at your expense. Are they really on your side? Are they really looking to maximize the value of your shares or just the value to themselves?

THE BFMA OFFER IS REAL AND CREDIBLE
MR. STANLEY CLAIMS: "BFMA has never made a formal offer to acquire Guest Supply and has not demonstrated an ability to finance a purchase at $21 per share."
THE TRUTH IS: On November 16, 2000, BFMA sent a letter to Mr. Stanley and the Board offering to acquire all of the shares of Guest Supply, at $21.00 per share in cash. What's not "formal" about that? In the six weeks since BFMA made its offer no one from Guest Supply has called to discuss the letter, even though we reached out to them a number of times. Despite what Mr. Stanley says now, BFMA has previously demonstrated to Guest Supply and its advisors BFMA's ability to finance an offer at a higher price than its current offer. In August 2000, representatives of BFMA arranged for Daniel J. Donoghue, a Managing Director of U.S. Bancorp Piper Jaffray, Guest Supply's financial advisor, to speak with BFMA's financing sources regarding BFMA's ability to finance a transaction at $24.00 per share. These sources indicated to U.S. Bancorp Piper Jaffray that the financing for the transaction was readily available.
Subsequent to these conversations, U.S. Bancorp Piper Jaffray continued to encourage the parties to talk without raising any concerns as to BFMA's ability to finance the transaction or the seriousness of BFMA's intentions. BFMA

is highly confident that it can finance its current offer. That is why we have committed substantial resources to encourage the Board to seek a sale of Guest Supply. BFMA has, in fact, received indications of interest and proposals from substantial and well-respected institutional financing sources for commitments in excess of $250,000,000.

MR. STANLEY CLAIMS: If BFMA wants to purchase Guest Supply stock, ... it is free to make an unequivocal offer based on the comprehensive information about Guest Supply that is publicly available ..."

THE TRUTH IS: We assume that Mr. Stanley is suggesting that BFMA make a public tender offer for Guest Supply's shares based on the information in Guest Supply's public financial statements. This statement is disingenuous in that Guest Supply has a significant number of anti-takeover devices put in place by management and the Board, including:

A Rights Agreement, commonly known as a "poison pill", which was implemented without shareholder approval, makes an acquisition of Guest Supply by a purchaser not approved by the Board practically impossible by permitting the amount of Guest Supply stock outstanding to be dramatically increased in the face of such a proposed acquisition. As described in Guest Supply's Annual Report on Form 10-K published last month, this acquisition-busting scheme automatically goes into effect "10 days following the commencement or announcement of an intention to make a tender offer or exchange offer, the consummation of which would result in the beneficial ownership by a person or group of 20%" of Guest Supply stock. In other words, once BFMA or any other would-be purchaser not approved by the Board merely announced its intention to make a tender offer to acquire Guest Supply, the poison pill would be triggered;

An 80% supermajority stockholder vote requirement for all business combinations effected without the approval of the Board; and A staggered board, divided into three classes which means that, even if 100% of the shareholders vote to change the Board, only two directors could be replaced at this meeting.

In addition, Guest Supply is governed by New Jersey law which provides that, without prior approval of the Board, an owner of more than 10% of Guest Supply's common stock cannot engage in any business combination with Guest Supply for five years. Therefore, even if BFMA, or anyone else, made any unequivocal offer, the Board would still have to approve the transaction in advance. To suggest that BFMA could buy Guest Supply without Board approval is entirely misleading.

If any potential purchaser were to make an offer without the benefit of performing at least some due diligence and without an understanding of the potential synergies, the offer price would have to anticipate the worst possible outcome. Management's unwillingness to cooperate with potential buyers serves to reduce the purchase price BFMA or anyone else would be willing to pay. This protects their interest, not yours. MR. STANLEY CLAIMS:

"BFMA is attempting to entice you to vote for its director nominees with an illusory proposal to purchase stock that may never be realized."

THE TRUTH IS: BFMA's proposal is not illusory. Evidence of BFMA's commitment is the investment of more than $5,000,000 in Guest Supply common stock and the expenditure of hundreds of thousands of dollars on legal fees and related expenses in connection with this process. BFMA has made it clear from the beginning that, if elected, the BFMA nominees will constitute a minority of the current six members of the Board. At least two of the incumbent members of the Board would have to vote with the BFMA nominees to sell Guest Supply. Is this what Mr. Stanley means by illusory? Is he telling us that, no matter how many shareholders support the exploration of a sale of Guest Supply, he and his Board will block that action? Vote for the BFMA nominees and tell Mr. Stanley and the Board to explore the sale of Guest Supply—NOW. Tell them you want them to commit to the prompt sale of Guest Supply to the highest bidder and to give ALL of Guest Supply's shareholders an opportunity to receive maximum value for their shares.

GUEST SUPPLY IS NOT REALLY
"EXPLORING STRATEGIC ALTERNATIVES"

MR. STANLEY CLAIMS: "In June 2000, Guest Supply retained financial advisers, U.S. Bancorp Piper Jaffray, to assist the Company in exploring strategic alternatives."

THE TRUTH IS: We believe that Mr. Stanley hired Piper Jaffray to stall our efforts. That is why he didn't let you know he hired Piper Jaffray or that Guest Supply was exploring strategic alternatives until BFMA's action forced his hand. In fact, during the nearly seven months since U.S. Bancorp Piper Jaffray was hired as Guest Supply's financial advisors, there has been no public announcement regarding any strategic alternative. After seven months you would expect Guest Supply to provide some feedback on its progress in exploring "strategic alternatives." What was U.S. Bancorp Piper Jaffray really paid for?

What other alternatives have they really explored or is this just another stall tactic? BFMA has learned from its discussions with industry contacts, investment bankers and other shareholders of Guest Supply that Mr. Stanley has consistently created roadblocks to having substantive conversations with other potential buyers as well. This leads us to believe that Guest Supply's "strategic alternatives" do not involve a sale of Guest Supply to BFMA or anyone else. We are convinced that the only alternatives Mr. Stanley, Ms. Unsworth and the rest of the Board will consider are ones that will allow them to maintain the status quo. BFMA welcomes a true, formal sale process in which all interested parties could participate.

BASELESS ATTACKS ON THE BFMA NOMINEES AND PRINCIPALS
MR. STANLEY CLAIMS: "Our shareholders should seriously consider

whether BFMA's nominees would be motivated to assure the highest price for
Guest Supply's shareholders, or—as we fear—the lowest price for BFMA."
THE TRUTH IS: While BFMA is very interested in acquiring Guest Supply,
we are waging this proxy battle to get Guest Supply to put itself up for sale to
the highest bidder. BFMA realizes that, in such a process, it may not be the
highest bidder and that if another bidder offers to purchase Guest Supply at a
higher price, BFMA will either increase its offer price or bow out of the bidding. Remember, the BFMA nominees would represent a minority of the
Board and it would require at least two other directors to effect any action.
BFMA and the BFMA nominees have not deviated from their request that
Guest Supply should be promptly sold to the highest bidder so that ALL of
Guest Supply's shareholders will have an opportunity to maximize the value of
their shares.

MR. STANLEY CLAIMS: "We are convinced that they [Logan D. Delany,
Jr. and Charles W. Miersch, the BFMA nominees] would not represent the
interests of all Guest Supply shareholders.... Messrs. Delany and Miersch
would be hopelessly conflicted in most important decisions of the Company
... they would have conflicts regarding their purported objective of arranging
for a sale of the Company."
THE TRUTH IS: If Messrs. Miersch and Delany are elected, they have
pledged to take all possible actions to maximize Guest Supply shareholder
value through the sale of Guest Supply to the highest bidder. As stated in our
proxy statement, they have both committed to tender their resignations as
directors of BFMA and Marietta, effective immediately upon their election as
a director of Guest Supply. They will therefore not be "hopelessly conflicted"
from serving as directors of Guest Supply and to suggest otherwise is misleading. In fact, given Mr. Stanley's own actions, it is offensive and hypocritical
that he would allege that these two upstanding and prominent citizens would
do anything other than fulfill their fiduciary and other duties to the shareholders of Guest Supply.
We note again that, if Messrs. Miersch and Delany are elected, the BFMA
nominees will constitute a minority of the current six members of the Board.
Accordingly, the BFMA nominees would not be in a position, without the
support of at least two other members of the Board, to effect any action.
Messrs.
Delany and Miersch have indicated that, subject to their fiduciary duties to
Guest Supply's shareholders, they will seek to convince other members of the
Board to vote with them to form a Special Committee of the Board and hire
independent financial and legal advisors to arrange a prompt sale of Guest
Supply to the highest bidder and on the most favorable terms available to
Guest Supply. So, it is unclear why Mr. Stanley is "convinced" that Messrs.
Miersch and Delaney would not represent your interests as shareholders.
What is perfectly clear is that the incumbent Board has not done a good job of
representing your interests as shareholders—of maximizing the value of your

shares—and that they are resistant to the idea of bringing people in who will seek to maximize the value of your shares.

MR. STANLEY CLAIMS: That Mr. Florescue [Barry W. Florescue, BFMA's President and Chief Executive Officer] has a track record of acting contrary to shareholder interests and for his own financial gain, which leads us to question his true motivation … BFMA has a history of decreasing its offer as a potential transaction progresses.

THE TRUTH IS: In his letter, Mr. Stanley had a number of uncomplimentary things to say about Mr. Florescue. In fact, he went so far as to use your money to pay Forbes Magazine an estimated $10,000-$20,000 to reprint and distribute a 13 year old article about Mr. Florescue's activities at an unrelated company.

We believe that Mr. Stanley's attacks against Mr. Florescue are a costly distraction and are unwarranted. Not only is Mr. Florescue not a director of Guest Supply or a nominee to be a director of Guest Supply, but Mr. Florescue has a long track record of creating shareholder value. Anyone who wishes to review the track record of the company cited in the article distributed by Mr. Stanley will conclude for themselves that the shareholder value created by Mr. Florescue during the ten year period from his arrival to the date of the article far exceeds the feeble return to shareholders during Mr. Stanley's nearly fifteen years as a senior officer and director of Guest Supply.

In addition, BFMA has offered to acquire all of the shares of Guest Supply, at $21.00 per share IN CASH. Mr. Florescue's stewardship of BFMA, Marietta and other companies is irrelevant. BFMA is offering to pay cash at a premium of approximately 25% over the $16.75 reported closing sales price of Guest Supply's shares on the New York Stock Exchange on November 16, 2000, the day prior to BFMA making its offer. If BFMA purchases Guest Supply, the company would be privately-held and the current shareholders would no longer have a continuing interest in Guest Supply going forward. Furthermore, the alleged facts underlying Guest Supply's attacks on Mr. Florescue's activities with respect to Century Bank are misleading and incomplete. In February 1997, the OTS (the Office of Thrift Supervision) made certain allegations that Mr. Florescue abused his ownership and control of Century Bank (of which he owns 98%). In order to avoid the long and costly process of litigating and fighting with the U.S. government, Mr. Florescue signed a stipulation agreement with the OTS neither admitting nor denying any of their allegations and agreed to pay a nominal fine. Since that time, there have been no issues and Mr. Florescue continues to own the bank while remaining on its board and is the Chairman and CEO of the bank's holding company.

Perhaps Guest Supply is attacking Mr. Florescue because Clifford Stanley and Teri Unsworth will do anything in their power not to sell Guest Supply to BFMA, even if it means that they spend your money to retain their positions. Mr. Stanley cited BFMA's 1996 purchase of Marietta as an example of how BFMA initially made an offer at a higher price but actually purchased the company at a lower price later. What Mr. Stanley did not tell you is that Marietta's operating performance collapsed during their long and drawn out sale process over five years ago. Notwithstanding this collapse, BFMA continued with the process and ultimately purchased Marietta. A special committee of the board of directors of Marietta at that time received a fairness opinion rendered by Goldman Sachs & Company, one of the preeminent investment banking firms in the world, that the price per share that BFMA paid to the-then shareholders of Marietta was fair, from a financial point of view. As to the BFMA offer to purchase Guest Supply, BFMA decreased its offer from $24.00 to $21.00 per share for, among other reasons (a) BFMA being misled by management to expect better operating performance for Guest Supply's June and September quarters than were realized, (b) the offer of $24.00 per share being made six months prior to its current offer and at a time when public market and private valuation multiples were higher and the overall financial markets were not as volatile and © the delays by the Board and Mr. Stanley in moving forward with discussions over the summer. Even now, the economy has begun showing signs of slowing which will negatively affect the hospitality and lodging industries and the companies that supply them. Had Mr. Stanley and Ms. Unsworth cooperated with BFMA in June when BFMA made its first formal offer, you, Guest Supply's shareholders, may have well received your $24.00 in cash per share by now. Guest Supply's resistance to seriously discuss with BFMA its previous offer has cost you a great deal of money.

MR. STANLEY FALSELY CLAIMS THAT MARIETTA IS A PRINCIPAL COMPETITOR

MR. STANLEY CLAIMS: "BFMA is the corporate parent of our principal competitor in the lodging amenities industry ..."
THE TRUTH IS: Guest Supply is attempting to create the appearance of an issue when in fact there is no issue over Guest Supply and Marietta's competitive relationship. Guest Supply and Marietta are competitors. This fact was clearly disclosed in BFMA's proxy materials. What Mr. Stanley omits (and, apparently, would like you to forget) is that Guest Supply has repeatedly characterized its business as "highly competitive." In a highly competitive market, there is no significance to the competitive relationship between any two particular companies because there is so much other competition. Mr. Stanley also omits that the relationship between Guest Supply and Marietta is largely vertical. Guest Supply is primarily a distributor. Marietta is primarily a manufacturer. The combination of the two companies would provide for a clear vertical integration. Both companies do fill some small bottles and press bars of soap—however, based on the "comprehensive information about Guest Supply that is publicly available," Guest Supply only makes approximately $11.9 million of this product (as their inter-segment sales are publicly reported) which is only approximately 3% of Guest Supply's total 2000 sales. There are many other companies that fill bottles and press bars of soap. There

are many more companies, domestic and foreign, that could enter these markets easily and without substantial cost or effort. Furthermore, Mr. Stanley's claim that Marietta is already attempting to subvert any of the company's relationships is simply untrue. This "competition" argument generated by Guest Supply is a smokescreen hiding the real issue: management does not want to sell Guest Supply to BFMA or anyone else, no matter what the price or the cost to Guest Supply shareholders.

MR. STANLEY'S DECEPTION CONTINUES

MR. STANLEY CLAIMS: "We pursued our discussions with BFMA seriously, after over three months of effort, we terminated discussions for several reasons, including: (i) our concerns over BFMA's repeated requests for competitively-sensitive information while refusing to sign a Confidentiality Agreement, which it said on several occasions it would sign; (ii) the unresolved issue of how the transaction could be financed, particularly in light of BFMA's stated need to identify at least $10 million in synergies or cost savings to finance the deal; and (iii) a growing distrust of the true motivations of BFMA and Mr. Florescue."

THE TRUTH IS: BFMA agreed to all of Guest Supply's substantive requests regarding the provisions of the Confidentiality Agreement, so long as BFMA received sufficient information to be able to quickly evaluate the potential benefits of putting the two companies together. BFMA's initial request for information was made for materials that could not reasonably be used against Guest Supply in a competitive environment. We did this because we were aware of Mr. Stanley's purported competitive paranoia. At first Mr. Stanley agreed to supply a very limited amount of information regarding Guest Supply's business. However, even after numerous conversations between representatives of BFMA and Guest Supply regarding the information, Mr. Stanley refused even to commit to provide the requested information to BFMA despite the fact that BFMA would sign the Confidentiality Agreement. In fact, Guest Supply stated that it would accept less money from BFMA or anyone else rather than supply the requested information. As a result, BFMA saw no reason to execute the Confidentiality Agreement. In fact, had BFMA executed the Confidentiality Agreement, you, the shareholders, may not have known for another two years that BFMA made an offer to buy Guest Supply. We believe that you, as shareholders, should be appalled that the directors and senior management of Guest Supply were willing to give away your money in order to protect their coveted positions.

As stated above, BFMA previously demonstrated to Guest Supply its ability to finance an offer at a higher price than its current offer and is highly confident that it can finance it now. BFMA never stated that it needed to identify $10,000,000 in synergies or cost savings to finance the deal. It did, however, indicate that the amount of synergies it could reasonably expect would affect the price that BFMA would be willing to pay, given the cost of capital and expected returns to BFMA. Once again, Mr. Stanley "spins" the facts to serve his self interested objectives. BFMA has, in fact, received indications of interest and proposals from substantial and well-respected institutional financing sources for commitments in excess of $250,000,000.

BFMA has offered to acquire all of the shares of Guest Supply for cash.

BFMA's true intention is to pay the other Guest Supply shareholders a premium of approximately 25% over the $16.75 reported closing sales price of Guest Supply's common stock on the New York Stock Exchange on November 16, 2000, the last trading day prior to BFMA's delivery of the offer, and a premium of approximately 29% over the $16.30 average closing sales price of Guest Supply's common stock over the 20 trading days ending on the same date. What you should question is the true motivations of Clifford Stanley and Teri Unsworth, in not responding to BFMA's offers or in otherwise taking steps to maximize the value of your shares of Guest Supply.

WHAT ARE THE TRUE MOTIVATIONS OF
CLIFFORD STANLEY AND TERI UNSWORTH?

We question the commitment of Clifford Stanley, Teri Unsworth and the other Guest Supply directors to maximize shareholder value for all shareholders.

Mr. Stanley, Ms. Unsworth and other officers and directors sold personally-held shares of Guest Supply stock at prices below $20.00 per share in May and early June, at a time when Guest Supply had engaged an investment banker (U.S. Bancorp Piper Jaffray) to "explore strategic alternatives" and was engaged in discussions with BFMA regarding the sale of Guest Supply at a much higher price.

Why were these directors selling at prices below $20.00 per share at a time they were rejecting a $24.00 offer as inadequate and demanding $30.00 per share? Did the directors of Guest Supply have knowledge about the business that they were not willing to share?

Why were these directors trading at a time where they had material non-public information?

Do these officers and directors have another agenda other than seeking the maximum appreciation in the value of your shares?

During the period which Mr. Stanley, Ms. Unsworth and other directors were selling shares of Guest Supply common stock, BFMA was buying shares. In addition, by telling BFMA that it had to pay $30.00 per share but not providing BFMA with any information to help them understand why BFMA should pay that much was essentially saying "go away". Did we mention that last year Mr. Stanley, Ms. Unsworth and Paul Xenis, Guest Supply's Chief Financial Officer, arranged to have their personally-held shares of Guest Supply common stock repurchased directly by the company in the amounts of 120,000, 40,000 and 35,000, respectively? Ask yourself, why were they entitled to liquidity for their shares at your expense when other shareholders were not? In addition, management and directors have since sold and surrendered additional personally-held shares of Guest Supply stock at below $20.00 per share. BFMA believes Mr. Stanley, Ms. Unsworth and the other directors have been resistant to BFMA's offers because they realize that, in any potential business combination with BFMA, they would most likely no longer be officers or directors of Guest Supply. BFMA has learned from its discussions with industry contacts, investment bankers and other shareholders of Guest Supply that Mr. Stanley has had preliminary discussions with other entities with respect to buying Guest Supply. Yet he has consistently created roadblocks to having any real conversations with BFMA and the other potential buyers. It appears to us that Mr. Stanley, Ms. Unsworth and the other directors are only seeking a "strategic alternative" that keeps them in power—even if it means less value to you, the true owners of Guest Supply. Remember, they hired an advisor nearly seven months ago to explore strategic alternatives, and nothing has happened yet. Are Mr. Stanley, Ms. Unsworth and the other directors truly concerned with the best interests of the Guest Supply shareholders or their own self-interests? Decide for yourself what their true motivations are.

NOW IS THE TIME TO EXPLORE A SALE
Despite Guest Supply's reported record operating performance in fiscal year 2000, its stock trades at very low multiples of its EBITDA (earnings before depreciation, amortization, interest and taxes) and earnings per share. We believe that Guest Supply's poor valuation and low multiples are not temporary anomalies. Rather, they are based on the relatively small size of Guest Supply's total market capitalization, the limited liquidity in Guest Supply's stock, the poor communication by management with its current and potential shareholders, lack of research and sponsorship of the stock, and the cyclical nature of the industry Guest Supply services. We believe that these are unlikely to improve in the future.

VOTE NOW TO PROTECT THE VALUE OF YOUR INVESTMENT
Each Guest Supply shareholder has a clear-cut choice: vote for the two BFMA nominees who will attempt to convince the other directors to form a Special Committee to explore the sale of Guest Supply OR choose the status quo and allow management to continue to act in its own self-interest. Management's inaction speaks for itself. We believe that they are more interested in keeping their positions and perquisites than in maximizing shareholder value.
It is important to note that, after all of these months, Guest Supply's management and directors have failed to either deliver an alternative transaction or take any other major steps to maximize shareholders value. Their request that you stick with them is neither credible nor likely to result in a higher value for your shares.
A VOTE FOR THE BFMA NOMINEES IS A VOTE FOR SHAREHOLDER VALUE. IF YOU BELIEVE THAT GUEST SUPPPLY SHOULD EXPLORE A SALE TO THE HIGHEST BIDDER TO MAXI-

MIZE VALUE, YOU MUST ACT NOW! YOUR VOTE AND PROMPT ACTION ARE IMPORTANT. WE URGE YOU TO GRANT YOUR PROXY FOR THE BFMA NOMINEES BY SIGNING, DATING AND RETURNING THE ENCLOSED BLUE PROXY CARD TODAY. If you have any questions or need assistance in voting your shares, please call Innisfree M&A Incorporated, the firm assisting us in the solicitation, TOLL-FREE at 1-888-750-5834.

Sincerely,

/s/Barry Florescue

Barry Florescue
President and Chairman of the Board
of BFMA Holding Corporation

20

The Nightmare is Over

I considered the back and forth between Marietta and Guest Supply to be just background noise. I never believed that Marietta would successfully pull off a takeover of Guest. Having said that, I still believed this "noise" was crucial to forcing Cliff Stanley to either put together a management-led LBO that would have to top any low-ball Marietta bid or get a strategic buyer to pay even more. The key was that Marietta was keeping the pressure on Stanley much more than shareholders, like me, could ever hope to do.

As the year 2000 was winding to a close, rumors were flying left and right. The best source of information for me was from Paul Xenis, Guest's CFO. I had a much better relationship with Paul than with Stanley or Haythe, to say the least. While some shareholders were underwhelmed with his abilities, I felt he was honest, hard working and doing the best he could and that's all you could ask of someone.

While Paul never expressed it, I felt he had empathy for what the shareholders had endured over the years with their Guest Supply stake even though he disagreed with how our displeasure was displayed at times. I know he wasn't a big fan of the sarcasm I often used when I became frustrated.

Nevertheless, as time wore on, Paul also desperately wanted some type of transaction to occur. After all, he often took the brunt of the shareholder's wrath and he had some of the same financial pressure from the debt related to his option exercises as Cliff, although to a much lesser extent.

Paul and I talked fairly often during this time period and he shared with me the progress of the negotiations the Company was having with a very large strategic buyer. He never would tell me the name of the company. In mid-January, 2001, Paul told me that a deal was imminent, with only a few minor details plus completion of the paperwork standing in the way of an announcement.

Paul was more forthcoming with information than he had ever been with me during the prior eleven years. I got the sense that he was excited that the end was near and he just had to tell somebody.

On January 22, 2001, the eleven year nightmare was over. Trading was halted and a press release was issued announcing that Sysco Foods was acquiring Guest Supply for $26 per share, to be paid in Sysco stock.

I stared at my screen in stunned silence, only to be interrupted by all three of my phone lines starting to ring non-stop. I was relieved to hear from Sampson, Day, Emoff, Dolgin, Decesare and many others. It reassured me that I wasn't dreaming and this wasn't some kind of cruel joke.

Sysco Foods was a huge distribution company, doing close to $20 billion in revenue. Guest's revenue would make up only 1.25% of the total going forward. Sysco was an amazing Company. I think they had grown sales, earnings and their dividend for twenty consecutive years!

Once the stock resumed trading after the announcement, it immediately went to $26 on huge volume, trading hundreds of thousands of shares. I didn't know what was going on. Usually there is a spread between the final deal price and the current market price due to the time necessary to close the deal, such as required regulatory approvals and shareholder votes. The spread is due not only to the time involved but also to the risk that something could happen, causing the deal not to close.

The huge volume and lack of spread made me wonder if the market felt a higher offer was going to emerge from Marietta or someone else. I immediately called Rick Bloom and Barry Florescue at Marietta. They said they were not going to try and top Sysco's bid. They both sounded a little shocked and scared. I am sure the prospect of now having to compete with $20 billion Sysco, instead of tiny Guest Supply, didn't excite them.

They told me the trading volume and extremely tight spread was due to this being structured as a short-form merger. Basically, if at least 90% of the shares were tendered, payment for the shares could be made immediately, before any required approvals or shareholder votes. What I was seeing on my screen was the arbitrageurs buying up all the shares to make 10 cents, on a riskless transaction. They would buy Guest and simultaneously sell Sysco. There was no doubt about 90% being tendered because the arbs were buying up every share they could get and immediately tendering them to Sysco.

The next day, Marietta issued a concession letter to the shareholders. Here is that letter:

BFMA HOLDING CORPORATION
50 East Sample Road, Suite 400
Pompano Beach, FL 33084

January 23, 2001

Dear Guest Supply Shareholder:

As you may be aware, last night Guest Supply announced that it entered into a definitive merger agreement with SYSCO Corporation, in which each share of Guest Supply common stock would be exchanged for shares of SYSCO common stock worth $26.00. Although we are not pleased with the way that we were treated by Guest Supply over the past few months, the end result is not all bad. We commenced a proxy contest in November 2000 to force Clifford Stanley and his board of directors to pursue a process in which the shareholders, the true owners of the company, could maximize the value of their shares through the exploration of a sale of Guest Supply. We firmly believe that Guest Supply would not have been sold if we had not initiated the proxy contest.

The SYSCO offer represents a transaction valuation multiple of approximately nine times trailing cash flow. SYSCO's offer consideration is their own common stock, which trades at relatively high multiples for a distribution company. However, this would he a very high multiple for a cash buyer to pay. Our own financial discipline will not permit us to increase our offer without the support and cooperation of Guest Supply's board of directors and management team, which support and cooperation seem highly unlikely at this time.

During this proxy process, we communicated with the Guest Supply shareholders in a fair and honest manner and avoided any personal attacks **on** the principals involved. We simply tried to stick to our platform—force the board to auction Guest Supply to the highest bidder. Although we would have preferred to purchase Guest Supply ourselves, we feel strongly that the shareholders are better off now than they were before this process began. We therefore believe that it is unnecessary to continue the proxy contest and we will withdraw our nomination of Charles Miersch and Logan Delany, Jr. for the position on the board of directors of Guest Supply.

This process has been a costly and difficult one for BFMA. At first, we attempted to purchase Guest Supply on a friendly basis but quickly realized that Clifford Stanley would not entertain any transaction that did not allow him to continue in his current capacity, with Guest Supply operating "as an autonomous operating entity." We then moved on to the proxy contest. During this process, we received overwhelming support from many of the company's shareholders, our financing partners and our employees and customers. We appreciate all of your efforts and wish to thank you all for participating in this process.

Sincerely,

Barry Florescue

President and Chairman of the Board
of BFMA Holding Corporation

My next call was to Bob Shapiro. Needless to say, Bob was thrilled. Although his average cost was much higher than mine, he still more than doubled his money in 3 ½ years. I told him that he deserved much of the credit for forcing Stanley to finally sell. I felt the Shapiro's stock purchases added much more pressure on the Company than anything the rag tag mix of shareholders could have done.

Bob graciously deflected my praise and stated that it was his view that I was the key guy. The reality may be that both of us were important in laying the groundwork but that it took Marietta to get us to the finish line.

A few days later, I called Paul Xenis. He confirmed what Florescue and Bloom had told me regarding the short-form merger provision. He praised Tom Haythe for inserting that provision into the deal but then told me that the deal almost fell apart, at the last minute, when Haythe insisted on being paid his golden parachute! Amazing, but not surprising.

Paul explained to me the huge amount of financial data he was going to have to supply to Sysco headquarters on a weekly basis. He sounded surprised, but this is the kind of financial discipline that is required to consistently grow a company; like Sysco has done for over twenty-five years. I wish Guest had had some of this same discipline. They might have avoided many of the missteps.

I told Paul I appreciated his efforts over the years and wished him good luck in the future. I told him to call me if he ever got to Columbus. I really meant it.

I was in a state of euphoria for the next several weeks. I no longer had to hesitate answering my phone for fear it was another client wondering how much longer they would have to hold their Guest Supply position.

One of the things we always joked about during the many dark days we endured was that if we ever got out of this stock alive, we were all going to Las Vegas to celebrate. Later that spring, several of the money managers and brokers that were large holders for many years met in Vegas at the Mandalay Bay Hotel for a weekend of stories and a few too many drinks. Besides the core group of

Sampson, Day and Emoff, there was Dan Gallagher and George Burke from California and Sheldon Wilshinsky from New York. I thought about inviting Bob Shapiro but I didn't think it was his style.

Even though I no longer was a Guest Supply shareholder, I couldn't break my old habit of checking the bathroom amenities as soon as I checked into the Mandalay Bay Hotel.

21

What Might Have Been

The $26 buyout price was certainly a huge victory compared to the $8 5/8 level the stock had hit several times, over the prior several years, following some misstep at the Company. However, many of us felt that if the Company's contract business had been better managed, we would have been talking about $50 to $75 instead of $26.

Guest Supply's operating margin in its last year as a public company was 5.65%, a very good number for a distribution company. In fact, $20 billion Sysco Foods' operating margin was only 4.19% at the time. The problem was that most of us took our huge positions in Guest because we thought there was enormous profit potential in the manufacturing business. We never would have taken such a large stake in a low margin distribution company. The only way to justify owning a large stake in a small cap illiquid company is if there is the potential for a huge upside. This was possible from a high margin business, much more difficult from a low margin distributor.

We felt the contract manufacturing business could have big margins because all the fixed costs would be covered by the manufacture of soap and amenities for the hotel business so that the Bath & Body Works contract would generate high incremental margins. The general consensus among the large shareholders was that Cliff Stanley had been badly outmaneuvered by the more business savvy Les Wexner and his team at The Limited, BBW's parent company. The key point was when Guest spent $30 million dollars to expand and modernize the plant without first securing a contract from BBW guaranteeing volume and pricing; A monumental mistake by Stanley and the Board. The end result was the $30 million investment generated *negative* margins. The only thing that saved us was the phenomenal growth in the hotel business.

Wexner did to Guest what he had done to numerous other manufacturers in his apparel business. He would get a small manufacturer to become totally dependent on The Limited and then would squeeze them on pricing. His retail empire was largely built on the backs of these small suppliers.

This ruthless practice was fairly well known around Columbus, home of The Limited's headquarters. My error was in believing Stanley's assurances that contract filling was a Mom & Pop business consisting of a guy with a garden hose standing over a rusty old tank and that there was no one else that could handle the amount of volume necessary for BBW's rapidly growing business.

Even though I initially started buying the stock at $3 per share and received $26, the whole ordeal just wasn't worth it. It was a valuable lesson for me that fortunately turned out to be profitable. I realized just how fortunate I was to be out of this stock as the economy worsened over the summer of 2001 and the hotel industry slumped. I kept wondering what Guest's earnings would have been in that environment and where the stock would have been trading. Then came 9/11, only seven months after the buyout! The entire travel industry came to a complete halt. If Guest had still been public at that point, I am convinced it would have gone to $3, forcing me to sell my entire position, if there was anyone who would have bought it! I easily would have been wiped out financially. That's when I realized that no matter how smart you are, luck and circumstances play a much bigger role than I had ever imagined.

During the late 90's, Todd Emoff would constantly drive home the point that no matter what price we ended up getting for our Guest Supply position, we would never be able to make up for the gains we missed during the dot-com era. The market was going up 20% to 30% every year while we were treading water, stuck in our Guest position. I really couldn't argue with his logic at the time. We had fallen so far behind the market averages that it was difficult to imagine ever being able to make up that lost ground.

However, the market peaked in March of 2000 and plummeted over the next two years at the same time Guest was doubling in price. The end result was that we ended up more than making up the lost ground in less than two years! We thought it would take at least twenty years, if ever.

I received a package from Dick Sampson, shortly after the merger, which contained a framed chart that highlighted the point perfectly. It was a one year chart that plotted Guest's stock price and the NASDAQ index from March 2000 until March 2001. It showed the NASDAQ declining 57% while Guest increased 45%, a variance of 102%. The following phrase appeared at the top of the chart:

Always remember, just about the time everyone thinks you are an idiot, you probably aren't.

Dick always had a way with words, as evidenced by this phrase. I keep this chart on the shelf of the bookcase in my office. It's been a tremendous benefit to me over the years when things aren't going exactly as planned.

Another opportunity presented itself to us during 2000. Dynex Capital, a mortgage REIT that Todd and I had been in and out of several times over the prior ten years, had run into major problems beginning with the October 1998 financial meltdown. The Company had preferred stock outstanding that was trading at 20% of its liquidation preference. We felt that despite the Company's problems, the preferred would eventually be worth full value. Because of Guest's move up to the high teens, I had enough margin breathing room to load the boat on Dynex. We would eventually get almost eight times our money over the next four years.

All of this was happening while the market averages were still correcting from the huge late 90's run up. I actually had clients calling me to thank me for keeping them out of the dot-com mania. What a difference a couple of years can make in the investment world. As Dick Sampson said, one day you're an idiot, the next day you're a genius.

I don't think I would have survived the eleven year ordeal with Guest Supply if not for my family. When I bought my first share of Guest, I had 3 kids, all less than six years old. By the time of the Sysco buyout, I had five children, ages nine to seventeen. While my wife and kids had no idea what I was going through, all the responsibilities of parenting helped keep me distracted from my problems and more importantly made me realize what was really important in life.

I still keep in regular contact with Todd Emoff, Tom Day, Craig Decesare, Bob Shapiro, Brad Dolgin and Dick Sampson. I even get an occasional email from Rick Bloom at Marietta. One day in the summer of 2003, I got a call from Dick Sampson. He claimed he had the next great investment for us. A small publicly traded fast-food Company based in Denver. Dick went on and on, extolling the virtues of this company and how it was going to be a home run for us. The only problem was that it would be hard to buy due to its very low trading volume. As he was talking, I noticed out my window that the sky was darkening from an approaching thunderstorm. I didn't think much about it until I asked Dick to tell me the name of this Denver Company. He laughed when he told me the name started with a G, just like Guest. Just as he started to say the name, a big bolt of lightening struck my house and my computer and phone both went dead. If there ever was a sign from above, this was it.

978-0-595-51188-4
0-595-51188-0